Tess
CWT
2016

Difficult Children

There Is No Such Thing

An Appeal for the Transformation of Educational Thinking

by
Henning Köhler

translated
by
Joseph Bailey

AWSNA

Printed with support from the Waldorf Curriculum Fund

Published by:
The Association of Waldorf Schools
of North America
3911 Bannister Road
Fair Oaks, CA 95628

Title: *Difficult Children: There Is No Such Thing*
   An Appeal for the Transformation of Educational Thinking
Author: Henning Köhler
Translator: Joseph Bailey
Editor: David Mitchell
Proofreader: Ann Erwin
Cover: Hallie Wootan
© 2003 by AWSNA
ISBN # 1-888365-44-7
First published by Freies Geistesleben with the title:
   Schwierige Kinder gibt es nicht, 1999
ISBN #3-7725-1240-2

Introduction

At the end of the twentieth century, which has often been apostrophized as the "Century of the Child," a crisis mood is spreading with regard to the questions of education and upbringing; this mood is intensifying to Cassandra cries warning of an impending catastrophe. The uneasiness comes mainly from the fact that increasing numbers of children demonstrating so-called behavioral disorders are being classified as educationally difficult to manage.

Henning Köhler pursues the question: can children actually be spoken of as increasingly "difficult," or is it not the overall status of consciousness and of societal circumstances that is drifting towards a situation that is unbearable for children, just who or what is "difficult" here, anyway?

Köhler places accepted patterns of thought in question and outlines in basic characteristics a spiritually deepened concept of education and upbringing, which could lead us out of the current crisis of meaning.

From the Editor

The AWSNA Publications Committee is pleased to bring this second title by Henning Köhler to the English-speaking world. Köhler's common sense wisdom is most appropriate today when the nature of childhood is threatened and the kingdom of childhood cries out for preservation. The pathway to health begins with a restoration of our own sense of what is right and a reconfirmation of our own intuitive knowledge of how to be effective parents and teachers. This book serves as a guide.

Köhler uses extensive notes and footnotes. These can be found beginning on page 182. The footnotes are indicated by a numeral only while the eighteen notes are designated by a numeral followed by the letter "n."

—David Mitchell
Boulder, 2003

About the author: Henning Köhler (born 1951) works as a teacher of children with special needs in the outpatient practice of the Janusz Korczak Institut (Wolfschlugen near Stuttgart), of which he is a cofounder. He wrote the acclaimed book *Dealing with Nervous, Anxious, and Troubled Children* (AWSNA Publications) and several other titles in German yet to be translated into English.

Contents

In Place of a Foreword

Poem about Fright
(To Jessica and others)[1n]

The hill behind the house,
I heard it from you,
is the head of a motionless she-giant,
who fell over face first and since then
has been aerating the earth
with her breath, dream-
far. Her body has
collapsed in countless autumns and
rises and sinks in the birches.

Wind and stones in her hair.
You know what she is dreaming,
we know it not. You whisper
with the crickets,
the salamander guides you;
in full moon nights
someone must be with you, otherwise
you go and do not return.

Three machine birds
crash bellowing westward,
into the clouded red
of the dusking day,
three howling black missiles
emerge
in the evening color-dream
above the woods,
we watch bored;
for the threefold racing nothing
we have names and reasons,
for your fear
we do not
and throw to one another, we liars,
knowing glances.

Who still sees tumbled giants
at the edges of roads and knows
their dreams. A child,
who knows them, presses her fists
against her temples and screams:
you, torn from your reverence,
child of the crickets,
know no names and reasons
for the everyday inferno;
the breathsong
of your unmoving she-giant;
salamander child,
the lullaby that she loved
and in the birches rises and sinks
her secret song of comfort
of blossoming and wilting

abandons you; the sound
of her up- and down-
streaming life—fundamental resonance:
quiet-joy-resounding—
has solidified to eyeseeming green;
no more than a replica now, sight, object:
the harmonious beauty
—through which the wind whispers—
of the woods in which
she is dreaming.

Now you too see only the reflection
and hear only the echo of things;
now you too stand, in this second,
without
before the heaven-high mirror,
you want to flee, salamander child,
a different flight than your usual one,
you don't know whither, cricket child, you fall,
and I lift you up,
what else am I supposed to do.

We have mercy on you
and want to help you
become human;
that is our lie
for undesired guests;
I call you in secret human-in-spite-
of-it-all: despite everything humans
robbed from the human: too-soon-
human, too-late-human,
I do not know,

I only know: you are brighter
than the mirror could bear,
if you looked in longer than a second;
beautiful against all reason,
human being against all rules of the mask
game; in this vulnerability
we are not permanent residents,
here we become cold benefactors
and force you into our
dragon's bath of blood.

Part 1

⌐1⌐
Education and Upbringing:
The End of a Giant Project?

Why are there so many "difficult" children today? What can be done? Is it the children's fault? Can we blame it on poor upbringing?[2n] On modern living conditions? Parents, teachers and educators vacillate between self-reproach, mutual faultfinding, and accusations of adverse social circumstances.[3n] Some lament the deterioration of ethical values and wish they were back in earlier times; others say we need once and for all to shake off the old humanistic value criteria; their obsolescence proved well enough in the course of the twentieth century. The "cultural revolutionaries" of the sixties and seventies were actually deeply conservative. They were nothing but neo-romantics disguised as the avant-garde and trying in vain to uphold the myths of "freedom" and "dignity" against the relentless assault of Homo Oeconomicus.

There is a confrontation between backward, neo-conservative cultural criticism, with accompanying rumblings of an unmistakable reactionary timbre, and the post-modern lackadaisical "everything is okay" stance. The neo-conservatives want to reinstate discipline, order, patriotism, duty-mindedness, and honor—in short, the proverbial secondary virtues of civilization—to their rank of pedagogical leitmotifs. The rebuke commonly leveled at the post-modernists is that they engender a "new conformist, uniform archetype" (Horst-Eberhard Richter) [4n] of the consumer kid possessed by money, fashion, media, and sex appeal. They simply let this criticism bounce off them with a "so what?" Why rebel against the Zeitgeist if you can make pleasurable arrangements with it? What's the use of drivel about self-realization, a sense of reality, social skills, and so forth, in the age of personality fragmentation? The honorable, indivisible "I" has served its purpose, is used up, obsolete. The postmodern person is an "ensemble" of identities; the inability to distinguish between established and virtual reality is itself long since a given. The telecommunicative de-sensing of interpersonal relations, that is, the impotence of experiencing the relationship between "I" and "you," has become irrevocable. Thus reason the post-modernists.

This fork in the mainstream into two dominant directions seems to be hinting at something about the opinion-forming media. The one direction, uncritical, infatuated with technology, and hedonistic, is the "grand coalition of The Agreed" (Marianne Gronemeyer), along with its "esoteric" wing.[1] This stream makes fun of the way people can still be seen walking around in the educational landscape wearing stale libertarian [5n] modernist hats (such as creativity, autonomy, humanism, and so forth), which they moralistically pull over children's heads. The other direction is the neo-conservative rollback. This stream also cultivates libertine modernism as its archetypal enemy, but because of the ethical neglect that it allegedly spawns rather than its overzealous moralizing. In any event, the protagonists of the "Okay Game" (Richter) and the educational antique dealers are in agreement that the myth of "freedom and autonomy" is the culprit.

There is a large mass of people that is every bit as caught up in these problems as it is reticent about them, following the debates more or less uncomprehendingly, all the while struggling to come to terms with their children on an everyday basis. They seek out experts for advice; they skim the vast and contradictory literature on child rearing (which, as we all know, is enjoying enormous prosperity). And still they cannot get rid of the uneasy feeling that the whole battle of opinions out there in print merely revolves around the question of whether to plunge forward into the catastrophe, or pull back.

Education that conforms with the times, that just swallows (or even hails) all the dull-wittedness of plastic, television, comics, trivial pop, and computers with a lax "that's just the way the modern world is," spares the children no woes; on the contrary, it drives them straight to nervous despair.[6n] But the opposite conception, the unrealistic one that takes recourse to idylls that have never existed, is no better protection against restlessness, anxiety, fretting, psychological exhaustion and dis-orientation, those woes of the childhood soul whose epidemic spread is indisputable. These idyllists have nothing to do with the authoritarian activism mentioned earlier; rather, they can be recognized by their quite likeable but largely unfruitful inclination to solve the challenges of child rearing by seeing and depicting the world as harmless, sometimes to the degree that it verges on—albeit benevolent—deceit.[2]

Experiments in anti-pedagogy ("the best education is no education at all") have long since proven to be just as worthless as resorting to the restrictive arsenal of "black" education.[7n] The orthodox Left failed with its grand offensive to educate the masses. It had hoped that the problem of education would be settled automatically by concentrating on inculcating the working population with leftist ideology. These hopes, too, were dashed. The anti-authoritarian Left, to be sure, placed the child into the focus of educational thought, rather than into the need of "human material" for the economy. This cannot be praised highly enough; in practice, though, it never got any further than contradicting conventional forms. Its libertarian conception had no philosophical or anthropological basis, let alone a spiritual one, and so it was that the notion of an education towards freedom with expectations of partnership and autonomy placed on even preschool-aged children. This is another variation on the theme of pedagogical arbitrariness. Alexander S. Neill's ideas of an education toward freedom were misunderstood, as he himself lamented, as a call to programmatic neglect. But even the "authentic" Summerhill project lacked a fundamental cohesion that would point beyond the materialistic conception of humanity; and without such cohesion, any educational project must end up in a void.[3]

In summary, we must observe that at the end of the twentieth century, which has often been apostrophized as the "century of the child,"[8n] we stand once more at the very beginning in terms of raising and educating children. "Cassandra sits amid the dissatisfied, whether they are parents, teachers, or schoolchildren"; thus writes J. Fritz-Vannahme. He is trying to say that the mood of an impending catastrophe is abroad. Exaggerated? Not if we believe what we see. Gronemeyer proclaims "the failure of the school"; Neil Postman sees that "the end of education" has arrived; Winfried Dobertin has declared an "education emergency." "Don't lose your nerves!" Hartmut von Hentig frightfully cries into the rising chorus of those who proclaim disaster. "Education has always been a fundamental, personal, and highly incalculable challenge to grownups. Consequently, adults always suffer under their own failures in education or child rearing. In the face of the magnitude of the task, this is quite natural." True indeed. Responsibility for education does not go together with the concept of "Life Quality Lite." Children are no luxury article, no status symbol, no showpiece, no private amusement. Anyone wanting to do them justice needs to be to some degree long-suffering and capable of sacrifice, willing to confront his or her own weaknesses and reevaluate his or her living habits and outlook on life, willing not to just talk about self-education, but to undergo it.[9n] Sometimes people panic because of ambition. But nothing could make less sense than *running* an education as if it were a business project determined by a clear intention to succeed, and by means of the deployment—whether barefaced or more subtle—of cost/value strategies, to achieve a profitable final balance. Lamentably, it is precisely this nonsense that is part of a tacit agreement among society, the institutions of education, and the chiefs in charge of education and child rearing, i.e., the parents. It is a "justified risk," says the magazine *Zeit-Punkte* (February 1996) to initiate school reforms from the point of view of "gaining an advantage in the face of increasingly intense international competition."

Education as a project of the bureaucratic/industrial complex?

This pedagogically erroneous (putting it mildly) marching direction is foreign to childhood but plotted by educational policy. It is reflected wherever education takes its lead from the destructive ideals of societal competition and consumerism, such ideals as power, possession, and pleasure at the expense of others, sexual attractiveness, a worry-free and no-hardship life, and—only inasmuch as it serves all this—intellectual armament. Anyone wishing to dispute that these post-modern living preferences are "foreign to childhood" is admitting that until now they have neglected even once to observe a child with alert, empathetic interest. In order for upcoming generations, so goes the argument, to ensure power, prestige, and affluence for the "site Germany" in international competition, the upcoming individual must be armed for the ever harder competition for jobs and privileges, in short, with everything necessary to assert herself in the merciless contests of all kinds of egotism. Needless to say, argumentation of this kind leaves behind education and child rearing as formation of the heart, which is certainly no obsolete objective. Who speaks any more of the existence of a humanitarian impulse, a force impelled by ideals deep within every child's soul? A force striving to become more and more conscious and to do beautiful works? An elemental *need* inscribed in our very make-up as human beings, a need to merge our own development with the forces impelling culture toward a society formed in the sign of enacted love?

The present book intends to show that education of the heart is no pious wish, but rather an anthropological constant. Basically, most versions of pedagogical ambition is founded on failure to acknowledge this fact. Developmental psychology, which considers itself "scientifically rigorous," is not interested in hearing this, but wherever children are degraded to the status of an adult project and educationally driven towards a successful result according to measures prescribed by a success model, they are exposed in their property as incarnated beings of love to constant abuse. Public and private ambition join hands and generate an atmosphere in which children that counter the 'success model' can only be seen as living misfortunes.

We now stand before the remarkable and hardly coincidental fact that these living misfortunes are multiplying relentlessly, and gradually imparting to the academic discourse on education and child rearing an entirely unforeseen direction that is of little advantage to international competition. Childhood itself is revolting against the series-produced prototype developed according to the priorities of materialism and the market economy. In this regard, we are not only starting all over again;

rather, we find ourselves (in contrast to the euphoria over educational reform at the turn of the last century) before a situation of an altogether new kind. Is the "project" doomed to fail?

∼ 2 ∼
Psycho-Detectives and Pedagogical Mechanics

We need to become aware of a threat to consciousness. This threat is founded in the circumstances of our time, and it engulfs us all. It manifests in the increasing alienation between the world of the adult and that of the child. If it is true that today we "actually have a salvation to perform on every child" (Steiner, GA 296), it is because of a profound fear that sits in the souls of children stuck in a culture that closes itself off to the *inflow streaming towards us from the wellspring of childhood*, i.e., certain indispensable qualities of consciousness and impulses to give form. Inconspicuous children are no less in the grips of this alienation than the conspicuous ones; only the conspicuous ones are in our face about it and force us not to ignore it. There may never have been so many strong, courageous, light-filled children's souls descending and taking up the challenge of seeking their way in this world in spite of their fear and their alienation. Acts of *salvation* are what must be performed, not damage control. I will attempt to show why the difference between salvation and damage control is not just one of degree but of principle. I doubt that, as Gerhard Fels claims, "the anatomy of the child's soul has remained astonishingly unchanged for decades." That is simply impossible while the rest of the world has changed so drastically. Any *general* pronouncement concerning the psychological constitution of "the children" can only be made in reference to the state of consciousness *in general*.

We are virtually possessed by the penchant to place people in categories such as sick/healthy, okay/not-so-okay, of solid character/unstable, and so on, with regard to how they think, how they feel, and how they behave. The concept of "psychological illness" or damage exerts a peculiar fascination. "That is sick!" or "Doesn't that verge on being pathological?" are customary expressions that elicit a sense of having caught someone red-handed at being strange, perverse, or deranged. Use of such expressions indirectly puts oneself in the "healthy" camp. Educators and therapists become psycho-detectives who spy, gather clues, draw conclusions, and turn in the culprit, which of course is not the supposedly sick or disturbed child (who after all deserves our deep sympathy), but rather the pathological process plaguing her. The next question is then the one about appropriate measures. What great diagnostics we are! What connoisseurs of human nature!

Analytical vision fixed on dysfunction and inadequacy seeks to expose anything pathological in a child's behavior, i.e., anything that does not fit into our well-ordered world. This vision would seem objective and neutral, but it only *presents itself* as such. In truth, it is clouded by preconceived notions because it is obsessed with finding the perverse in the unique, the abnormal in the original, the deficient in one who is merely alarmed or perplexed. The concept of "pathology" applied here almost always has a materialistic slant (this includes the esoteric therapists): something "is not functioning right." I shall call this the *defectivist* approach to diagnosis of extraordinary character traits in children. This approach insinuates some kind of operational damage into anything it perceives as strange; such damage might be caused by poor upbringing or by other external influences such as heredity or even karma (yes, there is a defectivist, hence fundamentally materialistic conception even of karma). When this happens the child, the human being as a free entity with autonomous developmental goals, is eliminated—and it is likely *these goals* that are causing tension in the relationship between the child's I and the world. Any person who places himself at a *conspicuous* distance from mediocrity and enters into a strenuous confrontation with the world is ripe for measures that "in the end only serve the purpose of making a person docile and content with their white bread" (James Hillman).

If we could succeed in documenting this notion that the materialistic psychotherapist lacks care and "ethical imagination" in his study of the psyche, "then children could in many cases be preserved from growing up with the stigma of being 'abnormal'" (Ursula Nuber). But the dilettantism that betrays itself in the auto mechanic-type outlook on the course of childhood development has unfortunately ascended to academic renown. Therefore, it is not seldom that, due to the pressure exerted by such renown people, who otherwise would have vehemently rejected embracing a materialistic conception of the human being, often subscribe to such dilettantism.[4] Whether the symptoms children display result from suffering inflicted on them by and in the world, or from their wild originality, or from a nature that simply expresses itself in extremes, it is taken seriously when they are treated for these symptoms as if they were a damaged household appliance. If we lose our overview of a situation, we tend to long for a simple, clear-cut solution, and it is at such times that we are easy prey for this simplistc mindset. The *defectivist prejudice* toward "handicapped" children in the stricter sense is just as unacceptable, nay even trivial, in terms of a true notion of what a human being is. If we lament the application of such a prejudice on "difficult" children, we should draw no line of separation beyond which one is then allowed to speak of "defective people."[5] The autistic poet Birger Sellin ends one of his epistolary poems with the words: "Heartfelt greetings to you / from one who wants to learn / to be a simple human being." Behind this double entendre, Sellin is hiding the desperate plea *simply to be acknowledged as a person.* "I write for my mute sisters / for my mute brothers / let us be heard / give us a place where we / may live among you all," Sellin writes. When he uses the word "live" he does not mean a bed and a roof over his head, rather, how the so-called handicapped and other exceptional people live in their hearts. Are they, as faulty specimens of humanity, mere sub-lessees, permitted to stay by grace?

Interlude:
The Little Scaredy-Cat, or Is Kai Disturbed?

Kai is just five years old, the second (wanted) child of very conscientious, loving parents. Pregnancy and birth were without complication. Kai was a healthy baby, but from the very beginning he had problems sleeping. He would scream the moment he was put to bed and only become quiet in his mother's or father's arms. His motor development went somewhat slowly but proceeded within tolerable limits (although he skipped the crawling phase, going directly from sitting to standing). His language development, however, went extraordinarily quickly. He began using the word "I" very early. Only reluctantly would he explore the world by sense of touch. Everything unfamiliar aroused suspicion in him, and whatever made him suspicious he would not take hold of, if it could be at all avoided. Thus he lived out his curiosity via his eyes; for the most part he *observed* the world at a respectful distance. His sister, three years his senior, is by contrast cheerful, carefree, and adventuresome. She had placed her father as the most important person in the world before she was two. Kai loves him but is more strongly attached to his mother.

"Kai brought his anxiety and fear along," his mother says today. "He is a spectator: attentive, *very* attentive even, but he always has his guard up. He behaves as if in constant expectation of some catastrophe." He is afraid of darkness, engine noises, dog barking, rain and wind, unfamiliar people and situations, falling asleep ("that's when the bad dreams come"), being alone, and even his own shadow. At home, he never leaves his mother's side; in kindergarten, he never leaves the teacher's side. Every night sometime between midnight and 2:00 AM he wakes up and seeks shelter in his parents' bed.

But Kai is a most imaginative child. He can play for long periods of time with great absorption and inventiveness; he prefers to play alone. He draws and paints wonderful pictures and loves stories in fairy-tale style. It is a dilemma that Kai is a very considerate child to whom it is important that he cause no one any consternation and at the same time it does not go unnoticed by him how his parents suffer on his account. He tries to "make it up" to them during the times when he is anxiety-free by being exceedingly helpful and by showering his mother, in particular, with expressions of love and gratitude.

Is Kai disturbed?

There are two basic possibilities in a situation such as this. First, one can deploy the defectivist prejudice and explain to the parents that the child is psychologically damaged because, for example, 1) his mother is holding him back through over-attention in the early childhood stage; 2) his mother is transferring her own unprocessed childhood anxieties to him; 3) his mother is unconsciously using him to avoid intimacy with her husband; 4) consequently, his father is jealous, and is involved in an unconscious power struggle with Kai, which includes the archaic humbling scheme "contempt of the son (heir to the throne) in favor of the idolized daughter"; and 5) all this is all the more devastating in consequence, because a boy of this age is competing with his father for the libidinous favor of his mother—thus we have an Oedipal conflict, brought to a head by various aggravating circumstances, including a wonderfully complicated yet vivid family dynamic, which, as is fashionable, can be traced back over two or three generations. Hence it is as clear as day that Kai is suffering under an environmental anxiety disturbance caused by upbringing errors committed by parents who themselves suffered a disturbed upbringing, as well as by marital/domestic tensions. His anxieties are the result of his living circumstances, because he himself is the product of his living circumstances.

This is only one example. The defectivist prejudice can also combine with other theoretical approaches. Irrespective of what explanatory pattern we use along the continuum between the extremes of the coarsely biological and the esoteric, wherever we use "disturbance" as the presupposition for a psychological examination, the tacit agreement holds sway that the child is a product of his circumstances, his upbringing, his past. Thus the human being is reduced to the *marginal circumstances* of being human.[6]

Another possibility is hinted at by Michael Ventura (in collaboration with James Hillman), who responds to the question, "Who is spoiled by whom in childhood?" as follows: "Forget the word 'spoiled'! Let us say instead that we are born with a destiny, an impulse. Let us say that we come storming into this world. Then the child draws others into its destiny; its impulse has an effect on the impulses of others. In other words, the child . . . causes a disturbance in a much deeper sense than that it merely cries in the middle of the night. The disturbance that people perceive when a child enters their lives is their feeling the pull and the influence of the child's impulse, of his or her destiny, which in the long run may have very little to do with their own." I know Kai, his sister and his parents well. It would be quite a stretch to explain him in terms of a family conflict and/or a flawed upbringing, but that is just what would happen if specialists with the corresponding *a priori* were to deal with his case. But Kai's story belongs with those stories that no one will ever understand as long as they refuse to make peace with the *mystery*, to distance themselves from the short-circuit conclusion that knowledge is synonymous with de-mystification. Whether we "know" more than the ancient mystics did about the moon now that we have identified it as a desert of stone and thus de-mystified it, or whether we know more than a future cosmology will, is questionable, to say the least.[7] It is no different with children, for it is just as questionable that more has been "known" about them since the successful assertion of the de-mystified conception that a primate species called the human being, which is in part genetically pre-programmed and in part formed by the environment, develops out of a clump of cells that has no identity and resembles a raspberry. James Hillman made a remark that I consider a decisive contribution to the reinstatement of mystery, of magic, of the *amazing*, which can influence us in our interaction with children like Kai. "In the core of our souls we humans are pictures [and] we must define life as an actuation in time of the original germinal image that *Michelangelo* once called the *imagine del cour*, the effigy in the heart." Let us hear a bit more from this psychoanalyst, who is a rebel to his profession:

This effigy, and not time, is the primary determinant of our lives. Time merely actuates it. Do you see what this means?

It means that our history is secondary or contingent, and that the image in the heart is primary and essential. If our history is contingent and not the primary determinant, then the things that impinge on us in the context of time (which we call development) are various actuations of the image . . . and not causes of our personality. I am not caused by my history—my parents, my childhood and my development. They are mirror images in which I catch a glimpse of my effigy. The task of life thus consists in bringing one's moments into harmony with the effigy, or with what was once called "guidance by one's Genius." Sometimes, the Genius seems to be making itself evident in symptoms . . . as a kind of preventive medicine that keeps us from going down a wrong path. Do you know how many extraordinary people have been runaways, school dropouts, who hated school, who were unable to adjust? The power of the acorn[8] allows no compromises with customary norms. In therapy, the riddle is not "How have I come to be where I am?" but rather, "What does my angel want of me?"

Hillman would surely agree that the gene, which has been elevated to the overall responsible party for everything that happens in the world, belongs in the "contingencies" category. On its quest for the *imagine del cour*, genetic research has ended up on a labyrinthine, false path. People will continue to chase the determinants of the determinants of the determinants until at some time (if we're lucky) there will be a loud bang, and we find ourselves once again standing in the middle of the *mystery*. The angel is no program; rather, it is the being that shatters all programming.

Looking back on the path of a person's life, the intentions of his or her angel can become discernable. But if it is *intentions* I am looking for, retrospection of this kind is a search not for causes in the normal sense, but for *traces of the future.* It is a quest for the "primary and essential" rather than the "secondary and contingent."[9] What consequences does this have for little Kai? If we do not see his fears as the result of unfortunate circumstance, but rather *seek* in them the veiled picture "of a final form that draws us on, a goal that exerts a continuous attraction" (Heinrich Roth), if we endeavor to construe his symptoms as "a kind of preventive medicine" that "keeps him from going down a wrong path," then the presuppositions on which our judgment is based change in the twinkling of an eye. We now take into consideration that his anxieties could turn out to be something *healthy*, or could be something that *ensures later health*, conceivably that in the garment of fear, Kai is rehearsing an attitude that one day will come in handy with what "his angel wants from him," provided it is given a positive turn.

I do not wish to anticipate the reader's considerations pertaining to this matter, but rather to suggest as an *exercise* that s/he fanaticize on the following questions: *For what maturing but still unrecognizable* abilities *could Kai's fearful disposition be fertile soil? For what* calling *might this fearful disposition be a preparation, in the sense that it has deterred him from taking a false path?*[10]

It takes practice to acquaint ourselves with this manner of posing questions. Without it, we cannot figure out what might have occasioned Rudolf Steiner to speak about the need in modern times "to perform a salvation on every child." If we want to meet the dilemma of so-called difficult children with an attitude of "productive love" which Erich Fromm, to paraphrase, would have said "combines care-giving, a sense of responsibility, respect, and a knowing understanding," it is not enough that we feel an amorphous pity, all the while looking at the supposedly disturbed child—albeit pityingly—as if s/he were an error on legs. The ability to devote ourselves to children in "knowing understanding" (in particular to those who put us most severely to the test), presupposes not just a few good intentions, but a fundamental transformation of our attitude. That is easy to say and—as I will demonstrate in the following—possible to do, albeit only through considerable effort.

⁓ 3 ⁓
In Favor of an Education
of the Heart

"This intellectual age of ours," says Rudolf Steiner (GA 306), "is too strongly oriented toward being right; we have gotten completely out of touch with our need to comprehend all things in life not just as *logically correct*, but also as *in tune with reality*." Paul Feyerabend, the anarchistic theoretician of knowledge who has unjustly been written off as a "philosophical scoundrel," underscores Steiner's remark by ascertaining that "purely intellectual solutions are not only useless, but harmful as well. They are useless because they lack the necessary concreteness. And they are harmful because today they. . . are forced on people against their wishes." Anyone who attacks academic science with statements such as, "Specialists are full of prejudices, they cannot be trusted," is either declared by these specialists to be incompetent, or, if that person's arguments are indisputably sound, they are somewhat more graciously branded as jokesters. The thinking *in tune with reality* that Steiner and Feyerabend demand is based on concrete elements, and thus cannot get stuck in theoretical generalities that merely satisfy our need for logic.

Reality-based thinking starts whenever one *allows the phenomena to speak* without having first plotted the frame of possible (or impossible) conclusions, and wherever one strives for creative formation of hypotheses[11] *without slavish adherence to convention* or to dominant habits of thought and judgment, but independently according to the criterion of how *sensible* it is. It is a matter of "raising the value of human existence" (Steiner, on the task of the sciences) through unprejudiced testing of thought possibilities that are worthy of being human, that is, which are gained from phenomena characteristic of *humanity*, rather than of the plant, animal, or machine world. This is where anthropology turns into anthroposophy. Anthroposophy places *central* rather than merely marginal value on facts such as the one that the human being is the only member of the kingdoms of nature to "possess" ego consciousness, and that out of this consciousness he is thus capable, in contrast to all other forms of life, of revolting against the conditions of his existence.[12] Anthroposophy realizes that full acknowledgement of such a defining phenomenon of humanity leads to an individual factor of development that is transcendent, i.e., *not subject to external circumstance.* Ignoring this simply because certain academic rules of behavior consider its mention offensive, is *unscientific.* The crisis of the times demands a different scientific attitude than the one that currently prevails. This different attitude would tolerate claims such as the one that the human being comes from nothing and disappears back into nothing; it would at the same time realize, however, that while such a claim can be championed as a personal belief it is *scientifically* uninteresting, because it is *senseless.*

It lacks "the necessary concrete elements." It is in a certain limited respect logically correct, in particular pertaining to material existence and the life of soul having to do with *it alone*; but it is *not in tune with reality*, because it neglects those phenomena that bear witness to the *spiritual* human being. "Sometimes one is stunned at the sheer intelligence [of natural scientific theories and procedures]; everything they do is right, but it all leads away from reality. If we want to raise and educate human beings, we must not depart from reality, because when we educate, reality is standing right in front of us; we have to get at the human being himself" (Steiner, GA 306).

Rudolf Steiner gives a *reasonable* image for the riddle of childhood. This riddle enhances "logical correctness" rather than denying it. He says, "Consider just once the degree to which a question [for example: 'Why are children today so difficult?'] shifts when regarded from this point of view: one could say the human being was in the spiritual world before he. . . descended into the physical world. Up there things must have been such that he was no longer able to find whatever his goal might have been. The spiritual world must no longer have given him what his soul sought. And out of the spiritual world the urge must have come to descend into the physical world . . . in order to look in the physical world for what could no longer be sought in the spiritual world" (GA 296). It is obvious that this child's quest is somehow connected with the educational "salvation" that needs to be performed "on every child" nowadays, in contrast to earlier times. What one needs to "consider just once" is not merely an interesting psychological footnote; rather, it places before us the *cardinal dichotomy of the science of education and up-bringing* concurrently with the turning point from anthropological to Anthroposophical thinking.

To the Anthroposophical way of thinking the child has a striving rooted in pre-natal existence. This striving is an individual goal for life that is not derived from any experience between birth and death. Rather, it has been carried into this life as the motif of a *quest*, and it influences the selection of experiences, as well as the processing and evaluation of incidental encounters.[13] Regarding these goals for life, *every* child is an intact and inviolable being. But circumstances can stand in stark contradiction to the impulses of one's destiny; events in life can become so overpowering that the actual determining entity withdraws in the face of them. *This* danger is greater today than ever; it is *from* this withdrawal that education and child rearing must "save" the children. What is it exactly that must be saved? The object of contention is the "impulse" that Ventura is hinting at when he speaks of destiny (that storms in), and what Hillman is referring to when he points to the working or, as the case may be, the will of the angel. Hans Müller-Wiedemann had just this issue in mind when at the first Conference for Outpatient Curative Education (1992), he addressed the "open mystery" of the *incarnation process*, that is, the arrival of a person on earth as the intentional *embodiment* of a being of spirit and soul, based on a pre-birth overview of that being's coming life. Müller-Wiedemann urged the members of this newly formed movement to make the "open mystery" the central issue of its theoretical as well as its practical work. By thus adopting the "open mystery," the movement could decisively offset increasing challenges by materialistic thinking to the dignity and full humanity of burdened (children's) destinies, and counteract the lifting of taboos on violations against the integrity of these destinies.

Today, chiefly for economic reasons, it is being analyzed whether the integrity of a human destiny (challenged or not) is not really a humanistic illusion that no longer has a place in our modern industrial society.[14] Setting up parameters for the value of life for the purpose of distinguishing between individuals who are suitable for human rights and those who are not suitable at all, or only to a limited extent,[15] is only the *boldest* consequence of what I have termed the defectivist prejudice, pedagogical judgment. One of the things that this attitude reveals, whether expressed with brutal openness or ethically embellished, is that today "intelligence has an inclination toward evil and is currently in a state of moral decline" (Steiner). This remark is not intended to brand any particular person as evil. Rather it pertains to signs of intellectual degeneration to which *all of us* are susceptible, inasmuch as we undergo a modern education which, to use Feyerabend's words, tends to produce one type of human being who has "many talents but no soul and no life." For example, the observation that our world is dominated by selfishness and egotism (is there anyone who doubts that?) is not an attack on any particular person, but rather a simple diagnosis of culture.[16] Perhaps one could begin by refusing this "decline" and breathing soul and life into intelligence. In reference to the topic of this book, the question arises, "What has to happen in order for education to get back its heart ?" (Steiner, GA 306).

Maria Montessori answered this question by saying that one needs to acquire the conviction "that the child already possesses a proper life of soul before it is born," and to ponder the concept of "becoming flesh" (incarnation). Hence one needs to consider that "in the body of a newborn . . . a spirit has become flesh, so that it may live on this earth." Montessori saw in this "spirit" above all the aspect of the Divine in general, but she also noted that it is the person's "own will that must help him become flesh." In regard to these questions, science still stands before "vast, unexplored territory." We recall that Steiner saw in the process of incarnation the *individuality* at work, which, to be sure, emerges "out of a divine world order," not as a separation of abstract cosmic energy, but rather as a kind of autonomous being[17] that sets itself goals based on its *own* destiny, even *before the separation*. According to Steiner, this setting of goals is something that "one must confront with timid awe." It is quite impossible to acknowledge the thought of an individual being that already exists before birth as a necessary prerequisite to each and every human birth, and at the same time conceive of education and child rearing as a gradual conditioning program for the purpose of training (please excuse the expression, but it fits the times) custom-tailored children, with the unavoidable consequence of categorizing them into quality gradations from well-made to inferior. Nip it in the bud! What starts with categorization of this kind ends up in "value of life parameters."

Maria Montessori, who instead of having her ideas taken seriously has been banned to the gallery of revered persons, wrote, "Everything that pertains to the soul of the child the adult judges according to his own standards, and this necessarily leads to ever greater incomprehension. From this perspective, the child appears to him as an *empty* being, that he is called . . . to fill with something; as an entity with *no inner guidance*, in need of guidance by adults. In the end, the adult feels himself as the child's creator, and he judges the good and evil of its deeds according to its relationship to himself. Thus the adult becomes the standard of good and evil . . . and everything in the child that deviates from the character of the adult is considered a flaw that the adult seeks to correct, post-haste. Through behavior such as this, the adult believes he is fervently, lovingly, and selflessly concerned for the well-being of the child. In reality, *he is extinguishing the child's personality.*" And Steiner wrote, "There is something in the human being that one as caregiver and teacher cannot comprehend at all . . . and that unfolds through the art of education, without him importing it into the pupil as a copy of his own capabilities" (GA 305). This is what needs to be saved.

Mariella [10n]

Something fell over your heart,
someone said: Cover up
your nakedness, and threw you
a nightblue cloak.

Now you want to be obedient,
so you can hear this voice's
tender whispering.
Only sometimes a wind of fear blows
under you nightblue cloak,
and reveals one of your feet.

Sometimes you weep,
not often,
not for consolation,
it just happens,
like rain comes down,
like tiredness falls over one's gaze.

Sometimes you hope that someone
will dare to take hold of your foot
and warm it at his heart,
not consoling, no:
demanding.

You will not submit to any warmth
that does not implore for your coolness;
your fear will only succor
who fears
your disdaining look.

That voice
that enveloped you in shame and homesickness:
Under your window
you want to hear it
sing love songs.

Too much you demand . . .
Perhaps there is one
who is invincible and helpless
at the same time: but this One
no one can possess.

⌁4⌁
Value-Discerning Vision,
or Why Parents Are Initiates

The practice of psycho-diagnostic categorization is rampant. Like many of my colleagues in child therapy and educational counseling, I frequently find myself in the position of having to caution uncertain parents against allowing their children to be classified by so-called disturbance profiles. Once parents are led astray in this way, they end up seeing their children with a subtle contempt.[18] By allowing thoughts and feelings of condescension to arise in them ("Why did *we* have to have a child like this?"), they miss a crucial—perhaps *the* crucial—part of their task as parents, which is to ease the harmful effects of the view that *evaluates* and *assesses*, by using instead a vision that *discerns value*. "Difficult" children are exposed to the evaluating, rating view everywhere. "Evaluating" and "discerning value" would seem to describe the same thing. Under closer examination, though, they turn out to be opposites.

The view that evaluates or assesses *always* does harm, whether it leads to positive results or not. This is because it degrades a person to the object of a quality rating. Anyone who for the purpose of being inspected gets reduced to a (lifeless) replica of herself feels a kind of pain that has to do with *shame*. Being fixed into a pose in this way thus hinders or even destroys relationships. It triggers an impulse to resist the anguish of shame, a reaction distantly similar to the reflex of wanting to hide or make a face the moment the shutter of a camera clicks.[19] "It is a fundamental truth of the human world that only an *it* can be ordered (rated, evaluated). A *you* knows no coordinate system," writes Martin Buber. The judgmental view forces a *you* into the world of *it*. On the other hand, *value-discerning* vision *heals,* and it does so not in the sense of treating a patient, but rather in the spirit of making one *whole*. The human being burns with longing for an answer to the question: Where do I find *wholeness*? Vision that discerns value addresses this question.

Modern language has replaced the concept of wholeness with that of dignity. "The individual *it* can become a *you* by entering into a process of relationship" (Buber). Something mysterious goes on when two people exchange looks. The very *wish* to see the other person as a *you*—that is, in her dignity—includes the fulfillment of that wish, because in my wishful effort to become aware of the person, I *esteem* her. Wanting to recognize a connection creates it. Vision of this kind is therapeutic—and thus understanding—in itself, and vice versa. The rating, estimating view stigmatizes in a way that increases the need for therapy, while at the same time impeding it. It throws its victim back into an attitude of *senseless acknowledgement* of the preconceived notion. The victim's sense of being hit by preconceived judgment actually contains its own defense against the interfering intentions of those who have scored the hit in the "deranged symptoms" that result.

We can substitute the word "pedagogical" for the word "therapeutic" in every instance here. Pedagogy means accompaniment in a helping, fostering way, and this is the literal meaning of "therapy." To educate (or to heal) is to cultivate relationships; one devotes spaces of time to it, but the effects of what takes place above and between these periods are subtle and far-reaching. Lamentably, even institutions that purport to perform spiritual pedagogy underestimate these effects with remarkable stubbornness, if they have to deal with disturbed (for so they are called even in Waldorf schools) children.[20]

The dignity perceivable to value-discerning vision cannot be described. It can only be experienced in a process of creative comprehending. We will discuss this more in depth later as a path that goes beyond the logical paradigm, but without abandoning it, and thus leads to an integral or intuitive [11n] investigation of an entity, or to the experience of *You*. Buber describes what one gets into in "creative comprehending" as follows:

"*You*-moments manifest in a firm and accessible chronology, as peculiarly lyrical but also dramatic episodes that are seductively magical, to be sure. But they are also of the most extreme danger, because they loosen the tried and true cohesion, leave behind more questions than answers, jar certainty and security. They are just as indispensable as they are weird."

James Hillmann calls this quality of experience "incredibly fascinating," saying that it forces us to the utmost at every moment. It always turns things upside down, demands the most radical thoughts one can think. It mixes up customary patterns of behavior and feelings. It would put the bottom-most at the top, so that one has to think in a revolutionary way.

Our biggest problem is our addiction to contentment. We just want to have things in a nice, neat overview. But on the interpersonal level, usual principles of order borrowed from the non-ensouled world are not merely inadequate; they take on "an inclination toward evil" (Steiner, GA 296). This inclination betrays itself in its push toward the categorical value judgments it passes on fellow human beings. One recognizes it in a pedagogical approach that is overtly or latently based on utility and function, in an inability or unwillingness to acknowledge the *You*, because this entails the eeriness of an encounter without reservation. Is such an inclination evil? Yes: it banishes love from helping, care-giving and healing, and it does so in order to make the life of the child's soul user-friendly for science and commerce. There is an obvious connection between wanting to satisfy an addictive demand for being on top of things and in control,[12n] the power of intelligence straying down the path toward evil (Steiner), and the current epidemic of autism, that modern-day occurrence involving a panic-stricken avoidance of unreserved encounters.[21] "Things and process limited by other things and processes that can be measured in reference to and compared with them create an ordered world, but an isolated world" (Buber). To place the child into *this* world as an object of our measuring and comparing is unworthy of humanity, whether we are willing to acknowledge it or not.

But let no one believe that it would loosen the tried and true connection of our superficial, measuring and comparing thinking in any way.

We would be fooling no one by acknowledging an inviolable or even immortal core of the human being in a non-committal way in *principle*, and then withdrawing in *practice* to the security of a "firm and agreeable chronology." From there we could resume our comfortable habit of evaluating under the dictates of a seamy concept of functionality. But even if we were to do so in the faithful assumption that all we were doing was forming an objective image of the human being, we could never rid ourselves of our tried and true superficial thinking, which operates based on measuring and comparing. Never. Not even if we were to talk about the sheaths all day long. You either dignify or debase. You either take up a relationship or break it off. Vision that takes up relationships heals; the view that breaks them off harms. The latter stockades the child into a version (!) of what it has become, and this version *is not its own*; the former turns to *that* future which *can* only be the child's own, and fetches this future into the here and now by "entering into the relational process." Some proponents of a spiritual image of the human being might make a better impression if they did not cultivate spirituality so much as a cosmic, overarching conceptual superstructure, but instead gave themselves over to the danger and the enchantment of "becoming an I by speaking *you*" (Buber). There is considerable *knowledge* to be gained from "shattering certainty" through rejecting the customary error of objectivity. Instead of cosmic dimensions jutting out of our cold intellect like monumental ice sculptures removed from real life or love, they emerge in our (thinking) experience in a quite unexpectedly *warming* way.

Spiritual points of view, I say, not intellectual ones! A matter is finished once the pertaining logic is finished. Spiritual truths are not finished once their logic is finished. Spiritual truths are ones that still need to go through life with the human being (Steiner, GA 306).

The unblessed alloy of addiction and contentment is an obstruction to spiritual truth. So are the intellectual compulsion to maintain order and the avoidance of nearness. These dominate interpersonal relationships today and with them the formation of concepts pertaining to the *Study of Man*. By nearness I do not mean indiscrete pressuring to get up close; rather, I mean the *you* experience as a higher sense perception.

These moments are immortal (and yet) they are some of the most transitory. No content can be retained from them, but their power goes into the human being's creation and knowledge. Rays of this power penetrate into the ordered world and melt it down again" (Buber).

Mothers and fathers are in a sense predestined to this quality in a relationship. They thereby open themselves to the danger of falling into an undifferentiated defensive attitude against *any* (even justified) concern on the part of outsiders, because they have a virtually clairvoyant feel for the proper entity of the child, which entity is still hidden and vulnerable. But that danger can be avoided by heeding the motives and attitudes of outsiders' input and only lending one's ear to those who lack self-interest and possess neutrality and sincere, warm-hearted interest. At the same time, such people will unquestioningly respect the fact that they have a deficit in the area of subliminal knowledge of the child beyond that knowledge of the parents.[22] One can sense this kind of nuance of attitude.

Quite often, though, we are faced by the opposite problem, that parents do not have a clue about their privileged role as irreplaceable persons of the child's confidence and as "initiates." Thus the possibility to make something of it is left fallow. The person the child chooses as the closest partaker in its destiny does not realize his choice status, so it happens that too many mothers and fathers "willingly accept the judgments that the child receives from others, such as kindergarten or grade school teachers." as Ursula Nuber regretfully ascertains, "and want the behavior of their child be changed and improved in the spirit of their demands. Rather than stationing themselves with self-confidence at the side of their difficult child, they gullibly accept the damage prejudice." But here in particular it would be important to take to heart how Jirina Prekop and Christel Schweizer express the parent-child relationship using the lovely image of the relationship between *guest* and *host*: "As a guest, the child must under all circumstances feel loved, must be understood, and be able to rely on her hosts. Under their protection, it learns to deal with fears, and to overcome crises and resistance."

Don't misunderstand: I do not want to rebuke parents, much less join the choir of those who right from the start interpret any sign of a child's suffering at the hands of the world as the result of poor upbringing or a lack of parental love. On the contrary, I am trying to *encourage* mothers and fathers to take on their privilege of destiny with gratitude and to defend it courageously against the arrogance of a ubiquitous "pedagocracy" (dominion of child experts and dysfunction specialists with academic degrees).[23] That is not to say that it would be wrong to obtain pedagogical advice from an expert or to get therapeutic help for a child. One can also turn to the appropriate person in the throes of one's own crises of orientation without relinquishing one's authority in the least. But if a person whom I ask to stand by me acts as if he were better acquainted than I myself with the world of my soul, thus when he brings his expertise to bear in an *intimidating* way and degrades me to the status of a layperson or even an idiot altogether, counter to my own innermost affairs,[13n] then there are two possibilities: either I submit to the advisor's verdict that I am incompetent and thus cease to believe in myself, and permit myself to be domineered from now on; or I energetically prohibit this kind of "help" and make clear that even if I ask someone to stand by me for the time being because I feel miserable, I am by far the best expert of my own life.

The same holds for the parents of so-called difficult children. *They* are the experts. Destiny has led them to an especially demanding task. They would be lacking in awareness of their responsibility for this task if they did not seek an exchange of thoughts with others active in the same or a similar field. This distinguishes competency from dilettantism, as does being troubled from time to time by doubts and fears of failure. Indeed, smugly knowing everything all the time is an unmistakable sign of charlatanry. That goes for educational advisors, teachers and other specialists in the affairs of childhood, *just as much* as it does for parents. Unfortunately, though, the abovementioned pedagocracy is a huge, elitist event that excludes the *true* experts, i.e., the mothers and fathers. They are crowded into the role of clients right from the start, as if parenting in and of itself were a predicament in need of nursing. Thus parents assume their calling with the feeling that they are not at all qualified for it. And this feeling is communicated to them by society.

The general contempt for parental confidence has evolved into a lack of self-confidence on the part of a large portion of parents, which in turn leads to uncertainty and pedagogically erroneous stances emerging from feelings of inadequacy. And all of this is in turn sanctioned by the pedagocracy. How can this vicious circle be broken? It might sound far-fetched to the unprepared reader if I say that parents need to regain their dignity as parents and that they can do so by acquainting themselves through the concept that children do not just come tumbling into this or that house, but that they deliver themselves to *those* parents whom they have *chosen*.[24] (This concept will become more plausible as we examine it from different angles.) From this vantage point, mothers and fathers are indisputably the primary responsible parties for education and upbringing and (potentially, at least) the most qualified chaperones for *their* children, and they should accept the judgment of only those who *share* this responsibility, or who are asked to give advice pertaining to it, or who acknowledge this privilege. They should also consider what the conscious affirmation of sovereign parenthood brings with it. Without a continuous and self-evaluating endeavor to obtain knowledge and to keep an open ear for heartfelt advice (or criticism) and genuine enthusiasm for the task he has assumed, no person can become an expert, irrespective of their field. This does not preclude crises of creativity. On the contrary, they are part of it all, for they uncover new sources of creativity. So it is in the art of education, just as in any other art.[25] "Today's parents will make many mistakes, just as their own parents made mistakes," write Prekop and Schweizer. "But that should not intimidate them. Without errors there can be no progress. Without problems there can be no solution." One could add that, in the first place, "errors" are not catastrophic as long as we are guided by a genuine and sincere effort to understand, and in the second place hidden forces take hold in such situations, and often in a way that what initially seems like failure turns out to be an instinctive act of good fortune in retrospect.[26]

Let us consider, though, that emphasis on the privilege of parenting and its concomitant responsibility does not mean that in the face of childhood crises we must blindly embrace the approach that *"anything* can have educational value." (I call this the imprint approach.) Parents do not make their child; nevertheless they are, as a rule, the most important people in the child's life. An educational task can (and more and more *will*) consist of using insight to receive the right impulses to action, so that as children's souls look out over their lives' paths fraught with obstacles, they are guided by the question: Where do I find the best stimulation to help me master the challenges and hardships that await me? In many cases, the tragedy today consists not in the parents of so-called difficult children being the wrong ones, but that they are the right ones and do not comprehend this due to the predominant modes of thinking. Thus it can happen that parents develop paralyzing feelings of guilt if their child has a hard time orienting herself to earthly circumstances, where everything would depend on them becoming aware of their *calling* to ease and soothe difficulties by understanding them. (Steiner and Montessori called such difficulties "conflicts of incarnation.") Many nearly hopeless escalations in misunderstandings in parent/child relationships stem from *this* central lack of awareness.

It is a risky business to accept literally the idea that parenting is a calling, rather than to acknowledge it as a mere metaphor (if at all). It is not only a risk, but a huge qualitative challenge to our thinking as well. After all, "as a person's intellect develops, it has a mighty inclination to become insolent and lazy. But it grows wings if the person feeds it with mental pictures gained from the spirit, which pictures can enter the soul only via the faculty of imagination" (Steiner, GA 305). The imprint approach can be of educational or genetic preference; either way, it is the fruit of thinking bereft of imagination. Steiner demands so emphatically that we "permeate ourselves with imagination" that it comes across as a categorical imperative. To mistrust the imagination out of fear of falling "straight into the arms of untruth," he says, is "cowardly with regard to the life of the soul." If this holds for education and upbringing in the home and in the school, it holds just as well for academic thinking in regard to education. We cannot send any observation satellites out into spiritual space, but it is possible and necessary for us to track down connections that lie outside natural scientific proof by using our imagination, which strives for *knowledge* and binds itself to moral *responsibility*. I am not talking about an out of control fantasy with no backup. I *am* talking about imagination, accompanied by clear thinking, as a power which enables *plausible* images that can be *confirmed through experience*. This power has always been an igniting force of the human mind at great turning points and breakthroughs. We need it today so that we can overcome the indolence within arbitrarily drawn boundaries of knowledge, so that spiritual ideas about the makeup of the human being can give us wings. The reality of these ideas cannot be *proven* in the conventional sense; the ideas prove *themselves* through their healing effects in the relationships from person to person.

I have already indicated the resulting methodological problems for obtaining knowledge. Vaclav Havel speaks in terms of "ideas that can endow us with an elemental sense of justice, with the ability to see things through the eyes of others, with courage, pity, and faith." Neil Postman's notion of the "crisis of telling stories," by which he means the banishment of sublime ideas to Disneyland, the realm of triviality, strikingly describes the imaginative vacuum that remained in the wake of the justified and necessary iconoclasm of enlightenment and today makes space for a new and living, image-rich language about the riddles of humanity. Regarding this, the issue of education is key. Anthroposophically-steeped knowledge of the process of incarnation, through which it is *conceivable* that parents are chosen ones, is the beginning of a grand, true story of childhood that for a long time was considered impossible. We will need this story. The human being is a storyteller, a weaver of words. As a word weaver, she is also a maker of worlds. World making, and not tool making, is what makes us first human, as Neil Postman says in refutation of a dominant materialistic theory on cultural development. Being chosen to be parents is an event. It becomes entirely true only when we see and recognize it, that is, when we comprehend it, when we grasp it as a concept. If everyone on earth were color blind, who would be willing to assert that colors exist not just virtually, but in fact? If we had not developed perspective, who would claim that three-dimensional space is a reality? An integral part of the reality of colors or spatial perspective is the fact that humans are equipped with organs of perception for these phenomena and with an ability to name them and, through the power of their thinking, to place them within the context of the world. To *think* individual preconceptional existence is in *this* sense to participate in its realization. The development of inner organs of perception for supersensible facts begins with us as "word weavers," fetching these facts into the conceptual fabric of the world. Naturally, the danger arises that old wine might be poured into old skins. Understanding the mystery of incarnation as a "sculptural" event and a process of initiation[27] demands not simply new *thoughts* but also new *movements* of thought. This will be dealt with in the following chapters.

The Art of Education: What Is It?

We stand in the face of a challenge that really wears us down, and also wears down the substance of our understanding of the world and humanity. Hartmut von Hentig (the one who cried out, "Keep your nerves!") is correct, make no mistake. Fear makes us lose our heads. But if the truth is so devastating that panicked reactions can simply not be avoided, how is one to remain silent or play it down?

Consolation and encouraging support *are* necessary, where it is a matter of individual crises (as with desperate parents, helpless teachers, sad children). This is what I as an educational counselor am called on to do every day. I do not presume to reproach parents and teachers who take their task seriously and still consider themselves failures. I see clearly how they are caught in the overall divergence between the needs of the child's soul and the development of society. The widespread conception of what matters in life needs to be comprehended as part of the problem of society. This notion of quality does not befit childhood; the superficial thinking about the human soul that accompanies it is thus also superficial as regards the development of the child. Individuals need reinforcement and encouragement in the face of this kind of thinking and these kinds of ideas.

But when it is a question describing the overall situation, mere consolation and encouragement are inexcusable under-exaggeration, and would be playing into the hands of those who have settled into the "okay morale," and lucratively so.

"Not even professional Cassandras . . . and experts in the field of education . . . who . . . still go at each other with the emancipatory and conservative verbal chaff of the 70s, succeed anymore in depicting the misery of education in a jarringly threatening way," writes Johannes Saltzwedel. Saltzwedel's distaste of "verbal chaff" is valid if one discounts the fact that it is gradually becoming boring the way any essayist or critic of current events who happens along tries to profit from being a part of the general thrashing of the idealistic counterculture of the 60s and 70s. Precisely such timeless qualities that are independent of changing trends of style can be more effectively defused using them in a ludicrous and inflationary way than through overt opposition. Nevertheless, Saltzwedel has no qualms about joining a miserable *Zeitgeist* trend when he simplistically pooh-poohs as a hollow formula the "emancipatory" notion as it pertains to the question of upbringing. Emancipation means liberation from forces that impede the development of the personality. Fortunately there are still (or perhaps once again) some warning voices that do not subscribe to the neo-conservative rollback and the post-modern yes-men, and Saltzwedel will have to reconcile his own journalistic conscience that he denounces such voices as "professional Cassandras," as if they could derive any advantage from warning of catastrophes. It is anything but advantageous to advocate emancipation and criticism of culture. To gain an advantage, one needs to flail away cynically at them with the intent of self-justification. Self-justification? The go-alongs and yes-men will not feel right about going along and saying yes if they are equipped with any intelligence. The critical, emancipatory stance has lately fallen into disrepute; that is why they reflexively turn this bad feeling against those unwilling to join the grand coalition of the agreed, even though they know better.

In other contexts Saltzwedel has contributed some truly intelligent thoughts, such as: "A different question has taken the place of the standard one about *how* and *why* children are to be educated, and that question is *who* is doing the educating, anyway?" Unfortunately, though, by conscientiously refusing to categorize the plight of our children as threatening, he is blocking his own and others' view of the facts. The situation *is* threatening, without a doubt, but threatening in a way that can be easily overlooked, as long as one keeps his gaze fixed on the barely passable external functionality of the educational apparatus. This is the only way *not* to either know the perspective of, say, the discreetly consulted child therapist and educational adviser, or want to make use of the possibilities inherent in an introspective study of man. The core issue is one of *quality*. This issue is drastically underestimated, and it cannot be circumvented by patronizing or appeasing.[28]

Bruno Bettelheim touched on the issue of quality when he wrote that "education and child rearing are tasks of creativity. It is more a question of art than of science."[29] The most wretched dilettantism dominates this art, whether one wants to admit it or not. This is not because of any ineptitude of individual educators or caregivers in principle, and not because of any lack of knowledge in the conventional sense. To the contrary, the growing host of specialists has obviously not brought us any closer to a solution of the problem of education. Rather, it is because one presupposes erroneous thoughts from the very start. The very way questions are asked needs to be reviewed, because it is based on apparently axiomatic things that are, in truth, fallacies. An example is the assumptions that the action of educating is arbitrary intervention into the soul of the child and that all that matters is *how* we intervene. Hence the child is a project on which we are working. It is possible to misunderstand the indication about education as a creative activity to the effect that the child is a lump of clay that the educator shapes, or a canvas on which s/he paints as nice a picture as possible. And of course what is meant by "nice" is arguable, since it is a matter of taste. What is a work of (educative) art that has turned out well? One can have varying opinions about this, but strictly speaking this is not the way to ask the question. The quality of an artistic event cannot be gauged based on whether or not a successful product has been achieved according to this or that criteria. The success of a work of art depends on what transpires between it and its observer, thus on yet another artistic event. Furthermore, just because a creative process takes place does not mean that a finished shape *must* emerge out of it. A finished product is secondary. The deciding factor is if the quality that appears finds a human being who understands it. In general terms, one cannot speak of assessment of artistic quality in any other way than in terms of the capacity to tell, through observation of the product, whether the producer understood it or not. Out of this understanding, a kind of care holds sway in the creative process, and this care imparts itself to anyone who makes an effort to communicate with the work of art.[30]

Thus the quality issue is an issue of *understanding*. The event of understanding is the artistic event. The person bringing something into an artistic configuration helps a possibility become a reality by inclining himself with understanding to its will to *become*. One can also turn it around and say that the artist helps a reality become a possibility. *Understanding presupposes the presence of what is to be understood.* Consequently, understanding is not an act of learning or of assimilation, but rather an act of discovering or revealing something that has already been learned or assimilated. What wants to *become* is active within me; otherwise I could not understand it. How does it get inside of me? Through the resolution to bring it into appearance. In abbreviated form, this means that the person giving something artistic configuration *remembers* what is yet to be brought forth, and thus makes it possible.

Children are not objects of our shaping or deforming activity. I am not only saying it is wrong to think so; I am saying that it is altogether impossible to do so. Whoever considers it possible has not comprehended the artistic feature of education, and thus the central aspect of the matter. It hardly needs to be said that there is little creativity involved in flailing about and waiting to see what comes out. But it might be less obvious that the artistic process, in essence, is no process of merely bringing forth some sort of structure that one previously bore within himself, and that one is now getting out of himself by imprinting it into some kind of matter, and so forth. The whole story about carrying something inside oneself and getting it out of oneself is distantly reminiscent of the childish superstition that the radio orchestra is sitting in the radio itself; the story's flaw is that people stop asking questions at precisely the point where things become interesting. Anyone who wants to get closer to the "mystery character of art" (Johannes Stüttgen) will just have to open himself to the fact that here something is happening beyond the customary context of causality. This is the paradoxical event of *an act of formation being caused by the shape to be brought forth.* It was not simply inside me or intended by me previously. The artist places herself at the disposal of a potential that is surging toward realization of a form of its own, and this *potential* owns the moment it becomes a *will force* to this encounter. Of course, potential should not be construed here to be a sense of contingency or possibility, but rather a super-spatial and super-temporal form of being, an *essence.* (Traditional works of art, for example paintings or sculptures, are entities trapped in solid forms, as it were, rigidified to hydrochloric acid.) The person who gives form incorporates, *is*, in a bodily sense, the dynamics of surging into, of growing into the reality of space and time. But he does not invent what grows in; rather, *it finds him,* as that person through whose understanding it can *create itself.* When the non-material passes through his body, it awakens to material possibility or, as the case may be, the non-sense perceptible awakens to the possibility of being sense perceptible and becomes an event on the physical plane. That is not to say that a mental picture or an image became symbolized. Rather the form-giver recognizes what has taken hold of him through its coming to manifestation, he is motivated *a posteriori*, or out of the future. What can aptly be characterized as creation out of a void from the material standpoint is a working essence out of the future, a turning inside-out of the configuration of time.

We stand before the phenomenon that "what is yet to be brought forth itself generates the very capacity that creates it. This is incomprehensible at first; it has to do with the origin of freedom, and it is how we reach the threshold" (Stüttgen). Any time and anywhere a person owns the ability to create to what is yet to *be* created, that person is—in the sense of this expanded concept of art—an artist. An artist of this kind discovers the *reason* to act in action itself, and the *capacity* to act in the future. This very kind of creativity is at the core of education relationships. It was what Janusz Korczak had in mind when he wrote that the educator "matures through the child toward the inspiration that educating demands." Steiner spoke of the "love for the very deed of educating" as the actual source of inspiration (GA 305). We attain true educational competency only when we as educators achieve our sense of self from an *experience of childhood* that guides us to the threshold. The issue of quality involves spiritually deepening the concept of the educator/student relationship as an art.

There is no other sphere of life where the process of "understanding confirmation" becomes more vivid. This process, outlined above, shatters habitual structures of thought. As an educator I help a (human) possibility to become a (human) reality, and vice versa; I do this by inclining myself with understanding toward the student's will to become. This understanding inclination is *the act of forming*; it is at the same time the only relevant form of educating. All actions and methods that seek to intervene in the traditional sense are qualitatively ineffectual. They *do* force the child to resist, and constantly being forced to resist can confound the will to self-formation, and weaken and clog it. Under certain circumstances, it can also fortify it in its resoluteness.[31] This makes it clear that the concepts of art and education, when thoroughly seen and thought through, reveal that education conceived of as a pursuit of *intentions* (even the very best ones) is just as dilettantish as passively allowing it to take its own course. To get to what is essential, we first have to become aware of the following paradoxical figure of thought: The child (his future *gestalt*) occasions and enables us to participate as guarantors in his self-engendering. The force that helps to shape is our understanding. The justification of my acts of understanding education lies in the acts themselves. Christian Morgenstern coined the concept of "creative, active comprehending." *I allow the child to take hold of me by forming herself into the space of my understanding. When the child does this, I recognize her individuality.* The capacity to act correctly, as the child wants it, flows to me from out of the future. Capability and goal are identical: there is no goal outside my capability, and I am capable of nothing contrary to the goal, because the goal is the individuality of the child. To her I owe the fact that I am capable at all of doing something for her. In the transition through the bodily symbiosis with the mother in pregnancy, and then through being interwoven in the supersensible corporeality of formative forces and soul shapes of the people to whom she entrusts herself, the spiritual and soul nature of the child awakens to its possibility of incarnation and becomes an event in space and time.

The point of view we gain thus is imaginative in nature; the first level of thinking as heightened beyond purely intellectual linking of thoughts. An entity (a child) raises herself to the shaper of herself by uniting with other entities capable of formation, entrusting her future to time, and finding herself (once more) in them. This union is an event of educative art: the child initiates the adults closest to her, to her innermost Holy of Holies, which is her future. But the initiatory knowledge she gains is not of the nature of mental images; it much rather endows her with ability. In this initiation lies the mystery of the educational relationship, which of course does not entail only pure bliss, but also a draining struggle. We will hardly advance to a living ideal of childhood that releases creativity as long as we plod along in the same old tracks of thinking. All pedagogical forming, even at the institutional and over-societal level, must be based on knowledge of the initiatory character of the educational relationship and of the artistic quality of its development. Regarding the issue of society, this means, to begin with, that institutions of education are essentially sites of initiation into the future of society. Adults become initiated by making themselves open for the pedagogical relationship as an art. The educators are the pupils in the proper sense. The social organism is laced with a network of initiation sites, a veritable irrigation system of work-shops in which the future is forged. This network is the sphere wherein creative processes of the substance of individualized warmth and movement (i.e., of childhood) interweave with the world of matter, structures, and death.

Obviously, any place can be connected with this network, as long as it understands itself to be a socio-artistic field of prac-tice. The force of childhood is not necessarily bound to bodily children, but is where children gather in body for the sake of initiating adults. The presence of the future is fulfilled as an event in an archetypal way. This is where the seam is. It means that working situations with the authority to set standards for the creation of social forms need to be instituted out of the field of education, and not out of the field of politics and administra-tion.[32] But good can come of this only if and when those active in this field actually comprehend the true tenor of their activity as addressed above. The current culminating issue of society is the problem that political and economic decisions have no basis in a real idea of childhood. Since these decisions are not being made out of the sources of humanity, they therefore have no socially artistic quality.

"If we discover the life of the soul in its true form, it is something creative, and at the same time the force that was ac-tive in our childhood as sculpting, forming activity" (Steiner, GA 305). This statement alone is enough to impart an entirely new direction to scientific thinking about education and child rearing. We are not dealing with some featureless thing to be formed when we educate; rather, we are involved with a *hoping* entity that entrusts to us the particulars of its hope and comes unto its own through our understanding. This entity comes into the here and now out of the future and presses toward its own configuration. It entrusts itself first to its parents, and then to other chosen ones! The event of birth is the arrival of an individualized substance of warmth and movement that achieves bodily being in the *temporal counter-stream*, and in the body folds back into itself as formative activity" directed toward the future. Incidentally, an origin out of the sphere of something yet to be brought about does not contradict the idea of previous incarnations on earth.[33]

Putting these phenomena into words "is like trying to paint lightning" (Steiner). But we must attempt it, because the Copernican Revolution of pedagogical thought that is due will only be able to take place if we first acknowledge that the enigma of humanity will always be overpowered by the logic of natural science, unless a different kind of logic, the paradoxical logic of the creative process, comes to its rescue.

⁓6⁓
Is Childhood Threatened
by Extinction?

The scope of education as an act of creativity calls for something more than just a series of self-evident observations. These observations demand to be circumscribed constantly, examined and re-examined from different angles; we need to pick up again on concepts already put forth and go into them more deeply. The linear, first-this-consequently-that mode of description is a most ineffective way to approach something we need to get to know gradually. To do this, we need to use the nomadic approach that children take toward exploring new terrain, i.e., to roam over it with no particular end in mind.

For the sake of further exploring this terrain, let us take another glance at the distinguished work of psychologist Ursula Nuber on the idea of childhood. Since I refer to Nuber on occasion, the impression may arise that my point of view and hers are identical. But they are only partially so. To be sure, hers is a carrying voice in the swelling chorus of those who accuse Freudian psychoanalysis of prejudice and one-sidedness, even of being a compilation of trivial myths.[34] She does dismiss the dogma that education and upbringing are an omnipotent influence on how a person develops. She deserves praise for that. Unfortunately, *fundamentally* she thinks of nothing more original to *do* with this insight of hers than to prolong the tedious, old dispute between nature and nurture. She shifts the weight back onto the gene and advocates "dispositionally caused" behavioral or natural peculiarities as the deciding factors in a person's inner makeup. She and I agree on the subject of tolerance, but not on pitting genetic determinism against the myth of the all-powerful "inner child."

I agree with Nuber that we ought not to attempt to turn a shy child into a gregarious one, or an overactive one into a quiet, thoughtful one. We are better off sounding out and *promoting* the merits of the shy or the overactive type of child.[35]

But why, when dealing with tolerance and respect of otherness, the genetic approach to an explanation is supposed to be better than the educationist model is a riddle to me. It is obvious that theoretically the tracks have long been switched in the direction of "preventive conditioning of behavior" through prenatal intervention into the genetic substance. This switching has been done in the hope that one day the primary task of prenatal diagnostics will no longer be to legitimize abortion, but rather to intervene genetically for the purpose of deterring a given disturbance, the goal being to ensure all parents of having "completely normal" children. The trend is unmistakable, and efforts to anticipate and calm ethical qualms are as considerable as they are hurried. But our task here is not to consider possible preventive measures to take against grave hereditary diseases; that would be the topic of another discussion.[36] What interests us here is that, given the opportunity to influence the bodily functions of a fetus in the womb, who displays the potential for hyperactivity, extreme anxiety or other so-called behavioral disabilities, there is no doubt that we would. The basic tendency to manipulate bodily processes in order to alter behavior or someone's character[37] already exists in the way we use drugs to treat any and every malady. Nuber laments that many so-called hyperactive children are treated with psycho pharmaceuticals the moment psychotherapists are at the end of their wits. She attributes this also to a rigid fixation on acquired behavioral patterns and/or to a neglect of an approach based on hereditary biology. How so? Psychopharmaceuticals influence the biochemical processes, which in turn affect the psyche. That means they temporarily "reprogram" the *phenotype* by means of a strong, externally administered, intentional influence. The "remedy" is given whether or not one knows if the biochemical processes to be altered are actually genetically determined, or caused by the environment, or by prior damage to the brain, or whatever else. Or if one does know they are genetically determined, the medication is administered with no consideration of their concrete genetic configuration. Finally, Nuber deserves praise for her stance on the four temperaments, which in her estimation are definitely not scientifically obsolete and do not merit being considered impairments even when they manifest in the extreme.[38] But her hope is quite naïve that "difficult" children will be more readily accepted when classified as merely "difficult in tendency."

The issue of difficult children cannot be addressed by shifting positions within the determinist paradigm, because the problem is determinism itself. As long as we see the child as a mere conglomeration of prior genetic and environmental imprints that is somehow barely held together by some ominous self-awareness that has cropped up, God knows when or how, there is in principle nothing standing in the way of the pretension to play fate by making even more intentional and, as the case may be, prophylactic imprints on the embryo. And all this is for the sake of improving the way children fit in with the already existing environment. All that prenatal conditioning would be doing anyway would be perfecting and consolidating the objectives of materialistic education and child rearing and their extended arm, child psychotherapy. Prenatal conditioning would eliminate in the womb what is disturbing and peculiar, with the regrettable side effect of the disappearance of all that is truly special.

Wherever there are signs of something special, they are signaled in a *disturbing* way. It upsets in a big way our bourgeois life with its comfy chairs of preconceived notions and carefully tended rugs of habit. The xenophobia of a world in which every thing needs its order does not go against only foreigners. It sits much deeper. As a socio-psychological phenomenon, it also hits those children who feel especially alienated in this world, and who—because they are incapable of hiding it—make an alienating impression on us. We need to make them feel *welcome*, which can be expressed in the following words: "I want to encourage you not to give up if you stumble. I know your path starts out in an unfamiliar land. But I know my way around here better than you, at least at first. I know that the customs of this land are still strange to you." Instead of being welcomed, they are restrictively naturalized, and I am referring to a restrictive *stance* that "means no harm"; on the contrary, it is widely considered to be the very ethic of social and pedagogical responsibility. But upon closer scrutiny, restrictive naturalization proves to follow from an opportunistic, xenophobic expectation on the course of children's development. All it wants is to help children adjust.

Perhaps we can account for the appearance of a new upootedness and home*less*ness in special children (Christian Bärtschi) through the fact that the home*land* does not permit anything special. In its rudimentary stages it impresses us as being peculiar. I will make a daring assertion: in the future, all education will be healing, healing in the sense of whole (Bärtschi). But that means that our task in the service of disturbing children is to *supplement*, for example by way of gingerly interweaving social skills into the child's so-called peculiarities, by being and providing good role models. How is a little eccentric supposed to learn to live with us if he detects that we are unwilling and unable to live with him? Word has gotten out that the pressure to assimilate exerted by "black pedagogy" cripples the soul, if it does not altogether produce living time bombs. Nor is it a secret any more that simply letting children do their own thing with no guidance (anti-education) is no viable alternative either. We have been through what we need to find out that we need a new, artistically educational mode of thinking. The present text is an effort to rehearse such thinking, which also manifests in the *curative educational attitude* put forth by Bärtschi. This attitude distinguishes itself through its affirmative, encouraging character, and in the way it vouches for the child in society and gives him advancements of trust. Most importantly, it shows consideration for the basic conviction of esteem on the part of the educator and caregiver, as a concrete factor of healing. What good are confirmation, encouragement, social guarantorship, and—what encompasses them all—*esteem*? In connection with his "extended concept of art," Beuys provides an answer that applies here: "The human being is not a being of the earth. He is in no way made for these earthly circumstances. He is only on this earth in part, for the sake of working on and through and out some very particular thing." Children perceive this strangeness of earthly circumstances with great clarity. Actually, what they want to do is return home. Yet they also sense that they have "something very particular that they need to work on and through and out."

For those so-called difficult children, which we prefer to call "special," this conflict becomes an ordeal, in one way or another. (It also becomes an ordeal for many an adult, but here we are speaking of children.) More and more, the world is changing in the aspect that a person is unwelcome the moment s/he *arrives*. To put it another way: the world is less and less willing to receive the impulse of childhood, whose regenerating breath is intended to blow away the stuffy gasses (Maria Montessori). But it *must* receive the child, so that it does not succumb to the aging times. The predominant forces that work intellectually, culturally, and socially are from the pole of death, not the personal kind that ends bodily existence, and are slandered today through the epithet of the "symbol of pure destructiveness" (Horst-

Eberhard Richter). Not death as a melting point and the site of the greatest mystery of life,[39] but rather death as a force field of cold, the force that causes deadening and in the face of which anyone wanting to work constructively stands stricken with profound fright. Within this force field is being carried out what I call the threefold loss of power. This loss is happening beneath the eyes of "the dominating euphoric alliance of positive thinking" (Richter). It is an expression of the separation between the human being and her extra-worldly essence (K. Graf Dürkheim). This triumvirate consists of the sclerosis of the imagination (death of thinking), the mechanization of relationships (death of feeling), and the utilitization (sic!) of action (death of will). It leads to, in terms of society as a totality, not only laying waste the (educational) environment, the legal system, and the economy, but it also leads with striking consistency to accumulating and using ever more catastrophic materials for the sake of explosion, deformation, and withdrawal.[40]

It is no coincidence that children are being exposed to a mind-boggling brutality of a new kind: they are being used, abused, and consumed in the consummation of a ritual of sexual contamination and mutilation of everything that is pure and innocent. This ritual is in part organized as a business and in part perpetrated by fragmented individuals. The *black initiation is taking place in good, civil families*. Often, a physical execution follows the psychological one. The virtually obligatory *filming* of such events is more than money making based on masturbation. Ceremonies devoted to the *murder of love* are being eternalized, multiplied, put on display. They articulate a kind of triumph. Child sexual abuse, burgeoning child pornography, pedophilic tourism, parents who rent out their children for prostitution—no sign of the times reveals the nature and effect of the force field of cold more joltingly. It is a matter of nothing less than the extinction of childhood. The sexual abuse of children takes place in an unconsciously symbolic, and hence ritualistic way. It paralyses the warmth impulse streaming in from out of the innocence sphere of pre-earthly existence by exploiting the core of the need for love and intimacy.

The threefold loss of creativity creates the climate in which atrocities are able to establish themselves as banal reality. Every year the mandated government report on atrocities inflicted on children shows a frightening increase—a new series of gruesome anecdotes over breakfast, this time child abusers. But what *really* lurks behind the mass offensive on the sphere of innocence, beyond obligation and horror stories?

Paralyzed imagination can no longer reach the picture of dignity, the image of *the child*. Surrounded by the mechanization of relationships, Buber's "you sense" or Steiner's "I sense" becomes numb. Direct, inspired experience of *you* is the source for intuitive acts of love, as is an imaginative vision for spiritual essences. But such deeds can only be performed within a space of freedom. The utilitization of deeds obstructs this free space. Imagination, inspiration, and intuition, as described by Steiner, are the metamorphoses of thinking, feeling, and willing, respectively. These higher states of consciousness are within reach of *you* relationships even today, and they directly oppose the stunted soul states of the threefold loss of creativity, constituting the "magic triangle" within which the idea of childhood awakens. They can unfold only in the striving toward the essence of childhood. That is why the essence of childhood is being so massively targeted by the forces working from the pole of death. The orientation toward necrophilia is out to get childhood and anything wanting to actively fashion the world out of the forces of childhood. Since the research of Erich Fromm at the latest, we have known that this is a diagnosis not of a mere individual pathology, but of an entire culture. It turns against the future, the principle of evolution, art. To make clear the actual trajectory of the "Ahrimanic offensive," we need to remember the connection of the quality "art equals the stream of warmth and movement" with the quality "origin out of the future equals childhood."

And we need to know intimately that the backdrop of these dark dealings is the mighty influx of a new experience of the Christ, and that it is this influx that is causing such a massive retaliation. Christ is the representative of childhood, "the Moving One" (Beuys). He is the One returning from the sphere of innocence as the shaper of ideas and the instigator to deeds that link heaven and earth, and therefore preserve childhood. And He is being greeted by an offensive from the counterforces.[41] This is why it seems that there is an unprecedented *dis*connectedness between heaven, or childhood, and earth, or the pole of death. (It not only *seems* so; it *is*, in a sense.) The child is "quaking in its alienation" (Buber). Everything depends on the number of people who verify with their thinking the love impulse approaching the earth, albeit never in a coercive way, and who turn it into will permeated with feeling. *This in turn depends on whether the idea of childhood is held firmly or not.*

Herein lies the devastating contradiction: the I drawn into a thanatomaniacal deviation loses its connection to the world, a connection which is established "between sleep and sleep in the lightning and counter-lightning of encounter" (Buber). This connection awakens the human being as a creator of forms, who forms *himself* into an entity of relationships and *the world* into a space for relationships. Being woven thus into the world we need a creative disclaimer or reference to the pole of childhood; we are exiled into the force field of cold and trisected into the three fragments of relationlessness (rigidified thought-person, mechanized relationship-person, utilitized deed-person). We are alienated from ourselves and the world, and we are at the same time at its mercy. In this way, we as captives know no reference back to the pole of childhood, and have no overview, no open moments of experiencing *you*, no liberated territory for tree planting initiatives.[42] This is what children fear and, nevertheless, what they expose themselves to, often in a touching overestimation of their powers and carried by a hope that commands reverence and a trust that ought to not just put us to shame but also to fill us with enthusiasm to do all we can to justify it in retrospect. Instead, the child who comes from heaven and is struggling to do justice to his origin, awakens to himself in our cold climes and all too often finds himself as "a pest who is looking for something but finds nothing for himself, who is rejected the very moment it enters" (Montessori).

The impulse of childhood—birth—is "an initiation for the purpose of movement," as remarked by Josef Beuys in reference to the Christ impulse. Movement happens in warmth. Thus it is the warmth-movement impulse overall that carries children into the world. It is creativity, or, we could also say, it is the current of individuality which always wants to soften and transform what has become solid and rigid. Hence we find ourselves in a deceptive calm and drifting toward a breaking point. We are confronted by the situation that there are children bringing to earth with them an ever-stronger warmth and movement impulse charged with the Christ Impulse. They have passed through Its sphere of influence before birth. So charged, these children are entering our disensouled culture of rivalry and into social circumstances that are increasingly frigid.

These words may sound peculiar, but we must create them and others like them and live with them, so that in the field of education we can evade the "dangers of the intellect left to its own devices" (Steiner). In the nineteenth century, Pestalozzi lamented the "living room theft" as a sin against children. "We have laid waste to and annihilated the living room." What the great educator said in reference to domestic life has lost none of its currency, but today we need to expand it to the larger picture. To be sure, these circumstances have in some respects become more civil. But as we have seen, they stand under the influence of forces that ruin interpersonal relationships and that are clearing the way for an under-cooled catastrophe, the main victims of which are children.

I am speaking of a drop in social warmth and of an impoverishment of spiritual movement, of the dictatorship of mediocrity, of the bored and cynical waste of the imagination and of relationships which can only flourish in the "mutuality of the spiritual life." Empathy will never rise out of the mediocrity of the intellectual soul. The Beuysian notion that "every human being is an artist" begins to become concrete wherever the joy of giving sparks artistic activism. Such joy can never overcome the drowsiness of people gathering together for utilitarian purposes. Where are friendships? Where are Arthurian brotherhoods? Thinking must become *bold* for it to become *good*; destructiveness demands neither daring nor mobility. Its products are grudgingly brooded out in the service of regulation. "It is natural that a culture as massively materialistic as ours generates materialistic behavior in its people, particularly in people with whom nothing more was ever achieved than the destruction of the imagination that this culture calls education" (Michael Ventura). How are children ever to find a home under such circumstances? They enter the earth with creative impulses that are repulsed before they even get beyond the stage of possibility. A deeper understanding of education and child rearing presupposes conscious verification of this "narrative" (as Postman would say). "Behaviorally disturbed" children are not "weak of ego"; rather, they are ambitious, even over-ambitious individuals, who have been *thrown back*. The following haiku by the Japanese poet Issa describes their inner state: "With new garments / I sit in front of the mirror / In solitude."

By the "attitude of curative education" we mean the artistic (!) endeavor to help children out of the solitude in front of the mirror by receiving with understanding the repulsed warmth/movement impulse, which at first makes them stand in the world like foreign objects. As mentioned earlier, this *esteem* takes place on different levels:

- We make the child secure in her feeling of her body and her existential configuration by means of our *affirming* attitude. A "yes" spoken deep inside ourselves invokes for the child shelter in and friendship with her physical existence.
- We intensify the "yes" to an encouraging and inner *comfort* (outer comfort is no use without inner), which strengthens the organization of the child's formative forces and gives her confidence in her capacity to give form creatively. We invoke the feeling of being at home in the sphere of life processes.
- Our *social guarantee* holds the child up and orders her as an entity of affect and emotion. But we can only make this guarantee if we project the "yes" into the future by and as a serene act of will.

All these are levels of love, and at the same time steps in an artistic, sculptural process.[43] It will become evident that this is no mere matter of words void of any practical bearing. What are the consequences if the opposite of these basic demands happens?[44] Wherever I do not approach the child by way of confirming his existence, I permit the feeling within me that he should not be allowed to exist the way he does, that, therefore, he ought to exist in a *different* way. In so doing, I ruin his fundamental bodily security and reinforce the experiences of alienation addressed earlier. Wherever I do not summon an encouraging attitude, I lack confidence in the child's autonomous forces of development, and thereby undermine his sense of self-esteem, causing in him an underlying feeling of failure. And wherever I deny him my social guarantee, I damage the foundation of trust with regard to his feeling held independently of any particular person, and abandon him in his loneliness and emotional confusion. *Esteem* is the inherent understanding that all of this is ultimately possible only if an actual *experience* of the warmth and movement impulse sets in. This evidence, this experience is the higher "I."

"To communicate the element of movement," says Beuys, "is the chief objective, as long as at the present time humankind lies in a profound state of paralysis." Beuys makes this statement without referring explicitly to the connection between art and childhood, but it lurks in the theory of sculpture like the flower in a bursting bud.[45] He continues: "I return to the sentence: In the beginning was the Word. The Word is a Gestalt, and that is the overall principle of evolution." What holds for "evolution overall" must also be valid for development of the individual. "We will feel and sense along with the child in a completely different way: if we always look at how the child is the continuation of something that could no longer remain in the spiritual world" (Steiner, GA 296). This is the incarnating individual Gestalt that is spoken into nowness and consists of hope.

These days people want to force special children, who often separate themselves for good reason, into social-ness by alleviating their individual particularities, socialness being what is left over. That is the educationist reflex, the unclear motivation guided by the orderliness of the mind soul, under whose coercive dominion we stand. Curative education, on the other hand, is a nurturing and caring attitude that takes its lead from the whole core of the entity, thus from the *dignity* of the child, from what it *is*, independently of genes and environmental influences, and in particular from what it *wants to become*. This is the way it *would* reveal itself if the world were a milieu of curative education. But the world is very far from being a milieu of curative education. In order for us to get closer to this goal at least, the thought must come to life in us that the human being actually is who he wants to become, and that every human being wants to become who he is.

In allowing this thought to permeate us, we create a milieu of curative education. It is irreconcilable with what we have called the defectivist prejudice, and it is so utterly irrespective of whether we ascribe the mode of behavior that bothers us to genes or to the environment. In the *Apocrypha* we find the following surprising sentences: "Wrench a person out of her circumstances and she will then be only what she is. But at times circumstance can bring something of oneself to the surface" (Beck, Dauber, et al.). We create spaces for this "at times" whenever we confront the educationist *and* (eu)genetic neglect of concepts and acknowledge the *difficult* child's inherent goal, her work in progress, what is striving toward a sensible realization" (Jeanne Meijs). Obviously, we ought to acknowledge the inherent goal of every child; but it is with "difficult" children in particular that we reveal the earnestness of our effort. "Children sense this. They are very sensitive toward adults and their surroundings in this regard" (Meijs). The shift will lead to nothing less than the "myth of the power and influence of childhood" (Nuber) having to give way, along with its psychoanalytic priesthood, to the "myth of the power and influence of the gene," along with its medicinal priesthood. And it is to be feared that the hurdle to treatment with psychopharmaceuticals will become lower, as the hereditary perspective gains an advantage over theories of trauma and suppression. Because in general, when one assumes psychological causes for psychological problems, one will likely assess the prospects for non-medicinal treatment as more advantageous than when one presupposes genetic burdening.

Adding a further century's chapter to the dispute over whether the cause is hereditary or environmental cannot increase our respect of a person's otherness. The new chapter will differ from the others only in its affinities and its epochal tint. Esteem will only increase when we acknowledge and take seriously that "three fundamental elements come together [to make up the human being]: genetic structure, the influences of society, and *one's own activity*, which implies that the human being has in part *created herself*." That is the first prerequisite to holistic thinking in psychology. But we must think beyond mere acknowledgment of the "power of self-creation" as just one of three converging elements. It is possible to do as we have done: to think it to the point where it appears *from* and *as* the beginning, as an *intended* force centrally linked with the I. It is not only possible; it is necessary if the thought is to gain the credibility it needs. There is no other way for the notion of *destiny* to enter our consciousness as that of *freedom*.

Face of Dusk
(for Sophie and others) [14n]

You stand at the window and your face is once more the face
of dusk, the foreign nine-year-old face.
Are you sad? I am afraid, as always.

Say something. Dusk has your face once more.
Why am I afraid. Won't you speak to me?
You stand at the window, I know the scene,
as if here inside were outside.

Like a homeless person who furtively
roams around the house of her longing.
You're freezing, I can tell by looking at your shoulders.
It's warm here. Well heated. I have to go.

Against this freezing
my fearful questioning is no help.
The mild irritation. The demand to be your comforter.
Your happy-maker. I have no right.

Do you need anything? — Don't know. No leave me alone. —
Why am I afraid.
As if somewhere out there, far, near,
your unreachable home were, your country of consolation.
If you need me, you know that. . .

As if the window were a glass sea and
beyond, close to touch, unapproachably far,
were your inside, your refuge. . .

How am I to describe your dark face,
your face of homesickness,
your forlorn nowhere-gaze.

Where do you come from? Whither do you wish yourself?
Where is behind the glass sea?
Where is nowhither?

Impatience breaks the vision for Whence Whither,
use breaks it, demanding
asserting, attaining, angst-haste,
what's profitable.

Where each of us lived in the time before his time,
where your lost nowhither gaze arrives,
where hope is air of breath, no, light of breath, where
you chose me and I recognized you,
there I could be with you sometimes
for a second of dusk,
if I could manage
to maintain silence,
to wait,
to allow.

⁊ 7 ⁊
The Future of Childhood and the Future of the Earth

There is an immediacy of the *"I –You"* relationship that requires the very creative potential of the human being as a bond between "warmth" and "time."[15n] Time is the element by which our existence unfolds, warmth is the medium that sustains relationships. But, as we have seen, "education as an art" [16n] is moreover a formational issue at the societal level. Society and the individual interpenetrate, and because we underestimate their interpenetration, the educational and socially artistic ineptitude [17n] results which over last two decades of the twentieth century have maneuvered us into a situation about which Cordt Schnibben says that "keeping silence has become the main form of societal communication." One by one the achievements of social and democratic government are being sacrificed on the altar of globalization. Ruthless worldwide competition among the rich for raw materials and sales markets is hampering the spiritual debate over societal questions pertaining to the future. The crisis of education belongs among the few truly weighty topics under broad and even sincere journalistic discourse; nevertheless the public debate is with few exceptions taking place at an inadequate level. Imaginative suggestions are downright frowned on, a reaction which has to do with the fact that we are unwilling to understand the problematic underpinnings of the nature of childhood. Instead, we erroneously believe that we need to proceed objectively, and that the only way to do so is to link it conceptually with economic and political exigencies.

What the issue requires, though, is not *objective* concepts, but rather *essential* ones. In the field of objectivity, i.e., in the arena of educational politics and the pragmatics of teaching and upbringing, the only thing that will prove fertile will be what we derive from listening into the essence of the child and the event of childhood.

To gain competency in the art of forming society, we have to dip into the future to get ideas for sculpting the present. But this future is not one that is hypothetically derived by prognostication based on the past. Rather, it is the sphere of what is worthy of striving within the dimension of humanity. This dimension can be grasped in the same intuitive way as one does a composition of ideas. This is the same artistic process as I have described for grasping the veiled future-gestalt of the child. The two questions of the formation of the individual and of society are inseparable because it is as undeniable as a natural law that *social developments are mistaken whose chief motivation is not to make childhood hope come true.* Rudolf Steiner's "fundamental social law," according to which in the course of history individuals have to submit less and less to social demands and society has to submit more and more to the conditions of the individual, says essentially the same thing.[46] After all, what Steiner had in mind when he formulated this state of affairs was not the triumphal march of egotism, but rather the *individual*. Only when the social organism is impregnated with the forces of individuality does it become a being capable of formation in an evolutionary sense. This impregnation occurs where educational relationships exist, *provided* a spirit holds sway there that does justice to the art of education as an event involving an initiation.

The directional impulse is *juvenile hope*. I have selected the term "juvenile" because of its dual meaning: 1) coming from the forces of youth, and 2) directly out of the center of the earth, the *spiritual* insides of the earth meaning those forces that have come to rest in all material formations, in every tree, every stone, every particle of dust. The mystery of creation is upheld in the center of the earth, as it is upheld within the core of the child's being, in the place where the adult stays a child for an entire lifetime, that is, in the depths of his or her heart. This is why hope owes its existence to the intimate understanding between earth and childhood. A social life worthy of the future is begotten in this understanding.

Children themselves are the only ones who can inform us regarding the directional impulse of juvenile hope. When the human being sets foot on the earth, she binds the design of her individual being with universal and fundamental prerequisites and expectations out of which she is born.[47] These are at once her source of and her link to an anatomy of child-like hope. If *we* now develop formative ideas out of an understanding of these prerequisites and/or expectations, we are practicing social art. Steiner shifted the concepts of Goodness, Beauty, and Truth, which have been abused to an unbearable extent, into a surprising and new light, by actually acknowledging that they possess "anatomic" characteristics of the childhood soul (GA 293). As thinking awakens, it is laid down according to truthfulness. It has neither encountered the lie nor learned the practice of lying. Similarly, feeling is laid down based on beauty—in the sense of dignity—before it is taken hold of and at the same time tempted by shame and outrage over the degradation and mortification of humanity by human beings. And willing is laid down according to goodness, before it comes into contact with hostility. These three qualities correlate to the core social requirements of freedom, justice, and solidarity. There is no other effective protection in the spiritual life (education, culture, research, teaching, and art) against the rise to power of the lie, in the instrumentalization of thinking, and in the imagination in the service of power interests, than unconditional freedom. Justice (equality/democracy) is an indisputable consequence that today's consciousness must draw from a heightening of the *You*–encounter. The latter has in modern times been elevated to the pure experience of God-likeness (beauty), through the vertical impact of the impulse of love from above, i.e., the Christ event. The equality of all people is no longer a question of assessment; rather, it is *evident*, that is, it is a perceptual content. This leads to the alleviation in social life of all privileges and/or hierarchical levels in legal standing and participation in the legislative process. Solidarity (brotherhood and sisterhood, helping one another) stands for the principle of good in the working world, hence where people act together in order to guarantee nourishment, housing, and care for everyone and to ensure the satisfaction of cultural needs.[48] Today, these core requirements are scorned as politically correct jargon, or at best they are revered as relics of a failed historical project. The disinclination towards big pictures that point the way into the future is coincidentally spreading proportionate to the inability to do justice to children.

Education is a central aspect of "social sculpture" (Josef Beuys);[49] in one sense it is *the* central aspect. Steiner presented fundamentals of this in his lectures *The Problem of Education as a Social Problem*. "The social question of the child," wrote Maria Montessori, "leads us to the laws according to which the human being is built." But she is not speaking of "laws" in the customary sense, not of limiting rules or unavoidable determinants. Rather, it is a matter of the mysterious event of formative forces intervening from out of the future and configuring the human gestalt as one of hope. The child is furnished with the capacity, the wish, and the drive[18n] to *develop herself toward* the Human Being, of *her* coming into being as an unique individuality.

Even this sounds paradoxical: self-realization is on the one hand the path of loneliness one takes in order to throw off "we"-ness in favor of "I"-ness; but on the other hand, seen from the spiritual point of view, it is the unfolding of the soul forces toward the archetype of the human being. This is bound up with the fact that the "basic word '*I –You*' (Martin Buber), which the Human Being speaks, cannot be spoken in a state of we-ness.

The development from early childhood to adolescence occurs in three steps, and it occurs as a *parousia* of the word as ground of the universe. The first years of human life are the fiery process of becoming upright, are imitative of the creation of the world and the wrathful awakening of the "I." Out of these—and this then makes up the center of childhood—emanates the warmth generated when one awakens to one's human dignity. And youthful idealism sets in when thinking opens itself to the future. The light of this kind of thinking transforms the respective carry-overs from early and mid-childhood: the elementary love of the world, which is of the character of willing, and the internalized sense of beauty create impulses for action. In these three steps, the child is not spared disappointing encounters with the respective adversary forces, the cold fire of hostility, the deceptive warmth of self-love, and flighty illusionism. But this connection of the social with the individual is a fundamental feature through which a prototype of the gestalt of the Human Being can be designed. The core problem consists in the adversary forces exerting a nearly unopposed hegemony. Hostilities, narcissism/egotism, and illusion are the structural elements of the predominant conception of the quality of life and certainty of existence.

The qualities of the sun (light, warmth, fire) that have been taken hold of by the I and become qualities of the soul are the "laws according to which the human being is built"; at the same time, they characterize the child's direction of hope, *every* child's. These qualities correspond to a threefold archetype of the social organism. The cardinal qualities in this archetype are freedom of the life of spirit (zone of light), justice and human dignity (zone of warmth), and a productive field (melting zone / fire zone) permeated with the will to help, with formative imagination, and with respect for the kingdoms of nature. One can invert the quote by Maria Montessori: the laws according to which the human being is built lead us to the social question; the social question is the issue of childhood. In other words, taking inner hold of the idea of childhood is for the art of social formation as indispensable as knowledge of static laws is for the architect.

Part 2

⤝ *8* ⤛

The Idea of Childhood
as a Factor of Culture

In light of the increasingly clear signs of the social cold front breaking in at the turn of the millennium, the question whether the idea of childhood can become a universal cultural and educational domain is of decisive significance for the course of the future. By becoming a universal cultural and educational domain, I mean the idea of childhood receiving wide acknowledgement as an overarching topic for formation of and within society. I do not believe that any other topic can revive the discourse on social ethics in the near future. In this overall climate of unwillingness to have anything to do with Utopias, no other ideal can be communicated that universally points beyond self-interest and the problems of everyday life. The idea of childhood is drawn directly from the sources of hope and human love. It is nevertheless not distantly utopic; rather, it is new every hour of every day. And what it more, it cannot be avoided. Children are entrusted to us. They are guiltless, vulnerable, existentially dependent on our understanding: there is no getting around them. The fundamental concepts of evolution, depth psychology, or the dialectical and materialistic view of the world were considered flighty and incomprehensible before they trickled down into the general awareness and became self-evident figures of thought found everywhere. In the same way, the idea of incarnation, the initiatory character of the pedagogical relationship, cannot but assert itself. Gradually, general acquaintance with the field of education as an art will either replace "common sense" notions as they become obsolete or add to them, inasmuch as they have any further potential. Of course, we need to allow for larger periods of time for this new orientation of thinking toward the *essence of childhood* to take place. But it is making itself noticeable everywhere as a vague longing. Over time, the idea of childhood will have to be pursued further and worked through in as many fields of life and knowledge as possible, such as medicine, sociology, psychology, philosophy and ethics, biology, history, and art. Today, and for a long time into the future, this application of the idea of childhood to the discipline is the link for making the quantum leap from anthropological thinking to Anthroposophical thinking as an overall attitude of consciousness rather than as a recent doctrinal edifice. It is the link for making ethical individualism, which contains palpably the idea of childhood, accessible as a challenge,[50] and for initiating a process of consciousness that leads to the notion of reincarnation, without it having to be proclaimed as a "theory." (Understanding the occurrence of incarnation is prerequisite to understanding the event of *re*incarnation.)

The idea of childhood is presented here in connection with the problem of so-called "difficult children." But it also has an intimate connection with Joseph Beuys's expanded concept of art, which stems from three things: first, both refer the human being to her creative source; second, both pose the question of creativity as an issue of consciousness, that is, as transformation of *thinking* rather than as the exchange of thought contents; third, both entail the social sculpture—the socio-sculptural aspect of doing deeds and creating works—becoming the actual object of all thinking, research, work and educating.[51] Every person is an artist, because he would be no human being if he had not, as an *entity of hope*, designed himself toward becoming the Human Being or, to put it in Beuysian terms, toward a society with the countenance of the Human Being. Each arriving child is this entity of hope in its purest intentionality. The expanded concept of art and the idea of childhood meet in the call to each individual not to betray who he himself is in his core, in the call to resist the influence of those powers whose destructive work more and more blatantly targets the center of human dignity. Thus, the offensive against childhood is at the same time an attack on creative individuality.

Suggestion for Education as an Art

Give your child something you yourself have made. Do this irrespective of special dates on the calendar, and *especially* when s/he is a problem child. The gift can be a fairy tale, a picture, a doll, a carving, or something similar. Or, simply give him or her time and attention: an hour set aside on a certain day each week, and shaped in a festive way. Not bombastically, but full of atmosphere, in a closed room, away from everyday doings in real, heartfelt togetherness, without stress or disturbance. *Dedicate* this hour to the child; dedicate *yourself to her*. Giving for the sole sake of giving, dedication for the sake of dedicating, are the best remedies against educative brooding and anxiously curious staring at the (difficult) child's behavior. Just say to yourself: "I have a *debt* to pay to this child—not because I have incurred debt with him in any mundane way, but because I have a reason to be grateful. Grateful for what? For this child having entrusted himself to *me*. I want to compensate my debt of gratitude by means of a genuine gift." Genuine gifts are *free* deeds of love in the way indicated: acts of forming a relationship out of the impulse of giving. The child does not have to prove himself worthy of these gifts; he *is* worthy of them. He deserves them, because he is there. But he will *feel honored* by this gift. And this feeling heals. *Giving and dedicating are fundamental motives of education as healing.* This holds not just for parents, but for the greater circle of those whom the child chooses to chaperone him through his destiny, such as teachers, godparents, friends, therapists.[52]

⮂ 9 ⮀
People or Plums?

Our habitual prejudices and systematic errors of thought are no minor cause of our children's peril. The central prejudice pertaining to education and upbringing is the contention of feasibility. Our more or less conscious point of departure is that parents and other persons responsible for education hold human fate in the palm of their hand; hence children are, with certain hereditary givens and environmental influences that are controllable only in part, objects to be formed from without. I call this the *cardinal error of educational competency* (see Chapter 10, "What is the Status of Our Humility as Teachers?" and Chapter 14, "Seeds of Acivity: The Poetic Path"). We cause much damage by doing nothing more than believing we are *entitled* and even *capable* of subjecting children to our intentions (which naturally are only the noblest). This attitude leads to lack of understanding between children and adults. Many children react to this belief with confusion, restlessness, distress, or anxiety. And then the vicious circle begins. The adults, under the impression of these *symptoms of alienation* in the children, become more and more entangled in the error of feasibility and resort to more and more unrestrained (naturally only the very noblest) procedures of manipulation. Manipulatory procedures do take hold; the screws of intentional, anticipatory education are tightened rather than loosened. One might manage to get children to adjust to these procedures, but this success is external only, and what the child experiences the most profoundly is that the longing he has been signaling for a *deepening of his relationships* has been entirely misunderstood, and requited by their being *broken off*. For it is a definitive breaking off of a child's relationship whenever the chosen companions of his destiny agree that the child has turned out poorly and now must be, as it were, conceived anew. The basis of trust is already swaying anyway, thanks to the illusion of feasibility; but it is undermined utterly by the decision to take special educational or therapeutic actions that are intended to correct a defect. That must be said quite bluntly. Difficult children open up an enormous *chance* if we *understand* that the message of their extraordinary features is a distressed question: Why do you not appreciate the trust I gave you when I initiated you into my secret? The only therapy that makes *sense* for so-called behaviorally disturbed children is a genuine *effort* on the part of those most intimately responsible for the child's education and upbringing *to muster an understanding*, and the effort to do so needs to be motivated by the insight that it is *the child himself* who has granted them the privilege of knowing his (the child's) secret.

Viktor E. Frankl wrote: "Parents give the child its chromosomes, but they do not breathe its spirit into it."[53] No, they do not do that; on the contrary, and herein lies the actual miracle that needs to be comprehended: the child breathes its own spirit into the parents (as well as into those who stand in close relationship with it, albeit without being blood relatives; these are no accidents). We are inspired out of the zone of the mystery and equipped by the child's angel with the ability to understandingly prove the truth of *this* child's unique entity and path. To make ourselves aware of this and to contribute our *true* strength (which rests precisely *not* on educative power) to the child, this is education as healing. But what do we do instead of this? We add to the habitual pedagogical prejudice of "feasibility" (all other prejudices arrange themselves around this one, as it were) the error in thought that education is as frictionless as possible a process of integration and adjustment that the adult is supposed to perform on the child. The decisive standard of human development that integration and adjustment presuppose is a developmental norm dictated by a conventional status quo that is strictly taboo. The goal of integration and adjustment is also *anti-individualistic* and *anti-evolutionary*. It rests on the misunderstanding that the process of individuation downright demands a more or less energetic *refusal* to integrate; such refusal is, according to Rudolf Steiner, the "antisocial" element that constitutes the basis of freedom. The human being is an *individual* to the extent that she does *not* subject herself to stipulations; she is a *member of a species* to the extent that she does. Both are necessary, but in terms of *education* one needs to make a decision as to what the main task is for today. "Education Toward Freedom" remains a hollow sound byte as long as in practice everything is set up with integration in mind, and the element of freedom is postponed to a biographical sometime, under the (false) presupposition that the greatest possible capacity to adjust offers the best support for the (later) autonomous formation of one's life. The refusal to adapt needs to be *creatively practiced*,[54] otherwise, "sometime" it will take on an uncreative (destructive) dynamic.

As long as we talk ourselves out of resistance to authority by saying that the issue of freedom is not even relevant before the coming of age, we are not taking seriously what makes up the initiatory character of the pedagogical relationship: the child has not entrusted itself to us as an entity of freedom (of hope) because we should or could "make" it free through this or that mode of influence, about which we believe that sometime freedom would come out the other end. That conception is pure materialism. Rather, the child entrusts itself to us so that we may honor the *act of freedom of coming into the world* as such, that is, so that we may be *permitted* to make it true through our understanding. By *protecting* in this way what is at once a beginning and an end, we are helping the child assert the motive of her arrival; we are the chaperones selected *for this purpose*. We have nothing whatever to make, not even to make the child into a free person. S/he *is* free. *Anyone who does not respect this cannot raise and educate children.*

The goal of assimilation and integration is *anti-evolutionary*, because it does not take into account the connection between individuality and cultural development, thus it refuses to acknowledge that, as far as cultural processes are concerned, children are the ones from whom *we* have to learn. We as administrators of the past confront them, who crowd in impulses of renewal (possibly radical) from the future. In children's behavior, even in their refusals, we can see harbingers of what is on the rise in the history of consciousness and what may yet overtake our current habits of thinking, judgment, and action. In other words, we have a golden opportunity to become *intuitively knowledgeable about the future*, that is, if we incline ourselves toward precisely the difficult children with a judgment-free and, above all, a *fear*-free thirst for knowledge, and if, through caring observation, we can see in the style of their refusal to integrate a statement about which new (social) abilities are needed in the world for healing development.

Just what do we base our judgment on when we isolate a child from the distinguished company of their peers? Let us not succumb to illusion here. We judge disregarding the individual, the evolutionary aspect, and the grace of being selected as educators. Jürg Jegge asks, "Toward what kind of concept of normalcy are we orienting ourselves?" He answers his own question: "It is a matter of the norms of the bourgeois school, and more broadly of the bourgeois society overall. [But] where is it written, anyway, how a child is supposed to develop, when s/he is supposed to be mature—a concept that is perfectly appropriate for plums, but hopefully not so much for people? And who determines that?" It is written in the literature of the pedagogical specialists, in the teaching plans, the parents' magazines and advice brochures. A truly ubiquitous expertocracy has taken control of the question of education and upbringing. The science of child development would be one of the most mature, if the equation "quantity + superficial behavior = quality" were valid. In hardly any other field are so many specialists so able to say precisely what is right or wrong, regular or irregular. To be sure, opinions are widely diverse, but all the same, the experts are multiplying relentlessly, the breeding of ever new (and ever murkier) disturbance syndromes, presumed causes, and methods of repair is turning into a national sport. Diagnoses such as slight autism, latent anxiety disorder, or attention deficit disorder syndrome can hardly go wrong. And in the face of this mighty specialized competency, pedagogical practice is becoming more and more unsure. Although we are so smart. Or maybe is it just *because* we are so smart? "I want to learn to love the wonderful creative 'I don't know,'" writes Janusz Korczak, and the thought comes from Grillparzer that "where wisdom is lacking, intelligence is a last resort."

Suggestion for Artistic Implementation of Education and Child Rearing

Try to *portray* your child. Imagine you are seeking advice about her from a certain counselor in whose judgment you place a lot of value, despite a quirk that for some reason s/he is unable or unwilling to actually see the child. Rather, this counselor needs detailed written notes, so that s/he can form a picture of the child. S/he has given you a certain amount of time for this task and warned you in advance that if the portrayal contains a single statement that is a presumption rather than a *pure observation*, if it is the expression of an opinion, an evaluation, or a conclusion, s/he will have to withhold all judgment. S/he is interested in neither remarks of praise nor of criticism, in neither interpretations of cause nor prognoses for the future, in neither analyses nor imagination. S/he is interested in phenomena only. You now proceed systematically. You make a plan for the time allotted you (let's say, two weeks), of the particular characteristics you want to observe on any given day, and in the evening you write down your observations. The memory gaps you notice will get filled in the next day. On Monday, for example, you might observe your child's facial features, her ears, the shape of her head, and her hair. On Tuesday, you would fill in yesterday's gaps, then observe her throat, the area of her shoulders and breast (form, proportion, posture), and her arms and hands. On Wednesday you would fill in Tuesday's gaps, then observe her breathing and voice; the next day her mimicry and gestures; the day after that the hip region, her legs and feet, her gait. Finally, you might describe your child's behavior during play (alone as well as with others) and during sleep, her eating habits, her agility and clumsiness, favorite fantasies and topics for conversation, and so on. Begin a journal. After a block of this kind, allow the matter to rest for a longer period of time, and then do this kind of portraiture once more, in part selecting new topics and in part resuming the ones you covered already. It would be useful if there is a person you trust who could hear you read from your diary and give constructive criticism about it: Are the observations *exact*? Are the conditions—i.e., no presumptions, and so forth—met? Mothers and fathers could alternate keeping the diary and reading to one another. Through pure, careful observation of the child's external appearance, that is, with no background thoughts and no commentary, her appearance will shine through for your intuitive faculty of comprehension. Gradually, something will enter your experience as the observer that emanates from the child as of a *light-filled nature*. You will begin to notice that you feel increasingly more certain in your daily interaction with the child. (Another suggestion that goes in the same direction, only further, will be described in Chapter 11) One can without exaggeration say that a kind of clairvoyance of feeling sets in through this kind of exercise in attentiveness, which is at the same time an exercise in *humility*. You throw everything overboard that you accumulated in the way of savvy (even anthroposophical savvy, as the case may be) and knowledge of people, all presumptions and rationale. The exercise will not work otherwise. Be reassured that such exercises are excellent for clearing out and ventilating that old attic of thinking. No one who wants to become intimately acquainted with the idea of childhood can be spared exertions in thought—that is quite obvious from a number of chapters in this book. But first one needs to take leave from one's accustomed intellectual posture and, as it were, start all over again: look, listen, ask, be astonished . . . and, last but not least, *dance*, which in the *Course in Curative Education* Steiner emphatically calls on us to do.

Excerpt from a Conversation:
Miriam M., seven years old, is described in a consultation as a disobedient, contrary, and obstinate child[55]

COUNSELOR: So there are clashes every day? No day without fights and tears?

MOTHER: Yes, it's terrible. She bristles at everything.

COUNSELOR: At *everything*?

MOTHER: At everything she is *supposed* to do.

COUNSELOR: But not against everything.

MOTHER: Okay, if we were only to demand of her what she thinks is fun anyway, then everything would be just fine, of course. . .

COUNSELOR: What matters is whether or not she can agree inwardly?

MOTHER: Yes. But that's exactly what she almost never does.

COUNSELOR: Give me an example of something Miriam does *not* bristle at.

MOTHER: If I were to say: Take your crayons and color a picture, she would be very happy. She really likes to color.

COUNSELOR: You're lucky there. That's a good sign. Do you call on her to color a picture on occasion? Do you *ask* her to?

MOTHER: That is completely unnecessary. She is constantly doing it anyway.

COUNSELOR: You should ask her to do it all the same. Say to her now and then: Miriam, I would like you to color a beautiful picture.

MOTHER: But what for?

COUNSELOR: So that she experiences that "should" can also have to do with nice things, and that there is not necessarily any contradiction between "should" and "want to." Otherwise, the conviction will become set in her that what is nice we *want*, and what is not nice we are *supposed* to do, and that is why "should" means "not want to," as a matter of principle.— Besides, it is a distinction for Miriam if you ask her to do something she likes to do of her own accord. It is an acknowledgement of her own will, of what *she* has to give. Creative activity is, after all, guided by the motive of giving, albeit subliminally.[56] When you signal that they are important to you by *demanding* Miriam's products, and then of course when you display your gratitude for them, you are strengthening this motive.

MOTHER: Good. To start with, I'll order a picture from her for the dining room. . .

COUNSELOR: . . . and have it nicely framed before you hang it up. It can also fundamentally do no harm if within your pedagogical relation with Miriam you invert the casting of "child requests /parents grant or refuse" once and a while. Now I don't mean these annoying pseudo-requests that are supposed to be an appeal to the child's "conscience." What I am talking about is *genu-*

ine requests, requests for something about which one knows: my child is drawing from *her treasures*; she has something to give. It is an unconscious arrogance that occasions us adults to crowd children into the role of the eternal petitioners. By the same token, it is a good exercise in attentiveness to ask oneself where do my child's riches lie? Where does she draw and give out of an abundance? One needs to learn to recognize and love what a child gives of her own accord and of her own substance, in a self-knowing way, and honor that by desiring it and asking for it. In general, it is just these riches that are not heeded at all, according to the motto: "That is nothing special. S/he does it all the time, anyway." Adults want to be respected or even admired for "what they do all the time anyway" (e.g., professionally). Why should this not hold for children as well?— Do you have another example of something Miriam does not resist, something she simply enjoys doing?

MOTHER: Stories. She drops everything she is doing if someone tells or reads her a story.

COUNSELOR: So if you would say for example: "This afternoon we're having a story hour," you would not expect any resistance?

MOTHER: Oh no. On the contrary.

COUNSELOR: Do you offer her story hours very often?

MOTHER: I read to her a lot. As a reward. Or just to get her to be quiet. She is constantly pestering me: Will you read me a story? Will you read me a story?

COUNSELOR: What I asked was if you ever *offer* her a story. For no reason. Voluntarily.

MOTHER: Well you know, she never lets me get that far. I use stories more as a kind of secret weapon against her obstinacy. With them I can get her to agree to do something sometimes. And as I said, she is always begging for them, anyway.

COUNSELOR: By secret weapon you mean that you say something like "Later, if you come inside from playing without yelling and wash you hands before supper, then I will read you a story"? Does she keep up her end of the deal?

MOTHER: More or less. I get pretty good results with stories.

COUNSELOR: All the same, you should *not* always couple reading stories with conditions, or wait for her to beg you for them. The same holds here as for what I said about painting. Call on her to come to a story hour once in a while. Without any catches or ulterior motives, but simply to honor her ability to listen. That is quite a skill, you know! It is a real gift. Do you have any idea how many parents suffer under their children not being able to listen to them?

More explanation of the principle of demanding / asking for what she wants herself, and some examples. . .

COUNSELOR: Earlier, in our conversation, we gathered a few observations that may be more important than they seemed initially. First, Miriam often likes to be creative. That shows that she needs to produce something beautiful of her own accord, to *give* something. Second, she likes stories, which means that she is a good listener. Third, if one appeals to this ability of hers to listen, she is willing to give in. Fourth, she does not bristle once you manage to get her inner approval. These are some remarkable characteristics we have collected here, and they are confronted by the huge problem that she constantly digs in her heels when you demand something of her of which she does *not* approve. Right?

MOTHER: Absolutely. And just this last point is what I wanted to talk with you about, and not so much about drawing pictures and telling stories. I agree that it would make sense every once in a while to ask Miriam to do something she likes doing. But the problem is that she *resists* all kinds of things.

COUNSELOR: It all belongs together. You only begin to understand when you look at the connections, and understanding Miriam is the most important thing. Because if you can understand, you can find your own best attitude towards the situation. In my experience, seeing a child's "difficult" sides in isolation and taking them out of context is a dead end. A "difficult" feature in a child only makes sense if it shows itself in the light of talents or other characteristics that we take for granted because they do not cause us any trouble. But if we look more closely, they are not at all that obvious; rather, they are quite noteworthy. *I* consider it highly remarkable that a child who obviously has a hard time being obedient in a certain way loves to *listen* (obedience, after all, does have something to do with listening), and at the same time senses a need to express herself through visual art.

MOTHER: Being obedient "in a certain way?!" Miriam is utterly and chronically disobedient.

COUNSELOR: Just a moment. You yourself made the qualification that she does not bristle when she can inwardly agree to something. Minding is not identical to unwilling submission. That is only the least invigorating kind of obedience. Let's assume just once the adult point of view: even dyed-in-the-wool fanatics of independence do not rule out *voluntary* obedience. It would be nonsense to be *forced* by the will to freedom into being disobedient. The inexperienced mountain climber obeys the mountain climbing guide as a matter of course. That does not hamper his freedom; after all, that is part of his decision to climb mountains.

MOTHER: And what does that have to do with Miriam's obstinacy?

COUNSELOR: She is constantly begging for stories. Strange as it may sound, that is her way of voluntary obedience, and it is up to us to translate it. We need to assume that by begging for a story she is bringing to expression—in code—the way she would need to be addressed in order for her to be able to be "voluntarily obedient" otherwise.

MOTHER: I'm supposed to dress everything up in stories? Telling her to brush her teeth in the morning, to be just a bit more quiet at the table, to get ready for bed at a reasonable time in the evening, to not go outside without a hat in winter, or not draw on the walls of her room? And so on and so forth? Are you serious?

COUNSELOR: No, I don't mean it quite that simplistically. Of course you *can* try replacing a command with a little story once in a while; that's not a bad idea at all. But I'm actually getting at something else. I said that we need to *translate* this strong wish for stories. Take it as an archetype: Miriam bristles when you tell her to do something, or not to. She does not want to mind. At the same moment, more or less, she asks you to tell her a story. She wants to hear, to listen, to follow. Now let's characterize the difference: within a certain scope, telling her to do or not to do something is inevitable, as far as the *matter itself* is concerned. But the fundamental tendency or gesture of a command is impersonal, cold, arelational or, if it escalates to a fight, aggressive. That's just the way it is. When you tell a story, though, you create a personal, warm atmosphere. Both have something to do with hearing, or following. An order or an injunction always evokes in a person with healthy feelings a more or less strong gesture of antipathy, and it definitely does so in children, even if they give in on the outside. A subliminal animosity against the person who gives the command or the injunction arises within the soul, quite naturally. That is no character flaw; rather, it is a reflex of defense against what is cold, impersonal, or aggressive, because one's own will is being attacked by something latently threatening; an element foreign to relationship is "disturbing" it. It arouses antipathy, which is perfectly normal. Except that not every child experiences this moment of inner defense with the same magnitude. Some accept it with relative calm. Others are frightened by it. No one knows why, especially when the animosity gets directed against the people the child holds most dear, such as mother or father. Usually, these children dig in their heels much less against other people to whom they have a more distanced relationship. . .

Mother: Yes, that's true. That's the way it is with Miriam, too.

Counselor: . . . and then that obstinacy comes out, which seems so insensible, but which is actually an outcry: I do not want to feel this animosity toward you! You always force me to reject you! Tell me a story! Now, let's just place both into a direct connection with each other: You always force me (to reject you)! I hate this mood that arises in me whenever you become categorical! Tell me a story! The mood that arises in me (toward you) *then* is nice. But that means that Miriam wants to *hear*, to listen, follow, to open herself. That is a downright irreplaceable element of life for her. She seeks the warmth of this special kind of togetherness, where she, by devotedly listening, is guided by you into a stream of pictures, an imaginative activity. Into this situation, she can entrust herself. She does not need to resist, and that is what she is looking for, really.

MOTHER: But I can't just always. . . .

COUNSELOR: Hold on for just a moment longer, please. Your story-telling has become functionalized. You use it to pursue a definite goal. Or you do it because you are forced into it, so that Miriam will finally be quiet. So the nearness Miriam is looking for does not even come about when you read to her. That is why she is disappointed every time and stuck with the feeling: That was not what I long for; something was not "right"; we need to repeat it.— I believe that her almost compulsive whining for stories has to do with the fact that the genuine story-telling mood only arises between you infrequently anymore. So two things would be important: first, that you implement story hours that are really free of purpose and intention, and full of the right mood (it might also be chat hours, during which time you could tell her about events that happened earlier, or show her pictures, or something similar); second, that you take to heart Miriam's "message" that she wants to open herself but cannot, that she has to close herself off against the cool objectivity (or reserved aggressiveness) of your command tone of voice. I suggest that her obstreperousness is the sign of an exaggerated sensitivity against her own feelings of antipathy, and when we give commands or make injunctions, we call this antipathy forth without fail. Paradoxical as it may sound, what really is hiding behind Miriam's constant resistance is a keen need for harmony. You need to do justice to that rather than getting entangled in the error of thinking (however understandable) that such an obdurate child must be of a spiny, contentious disposition. I swear to you that the opposite is the case.

MOTHER: To be quite honest, that is the way I have always felt about Miriam. What you are telling me is nothing new to me; only, of late I've lost faith in this feeling. How can I do justice to it?

COUNSELOR: It is one of my deep convictions that in principle no one understands better how to interact with a child than her parents. Whatever advice I give you is bound to fall short of anything you find out for yourself based on a true understanding of Miriam's nature. As an outsider I can help you to understand better, because my judgment is less prejudiced, from one particular perspective. But nobody can replace your intuitive capacity to do the right thing at the right moment. That is a talent that is specifically bound up with your (or anyone's) particular relationship. It grows if you cultivate the proper *thoughts* and get rid of preconceived notions that block your view of what really matters. We will continue to have conversations, but to start with I want to give you some homework. Whenever you have to tell Miriam to do something or to not do something, try to figure out how to say this to her in a way that speaks to her wish and ability to listen and be guided, and especially to her deep need for the mood of story-telling in mind. If you do it right, she will be able to accept what you tell her to do or to not do. Of course there will still be fighting, even if you gradually get better at this kind of mediating. Confrontations are part of the deal; children *have to* be obstinate; we must not forget that, over all the thought we put into the matter. But I am sure that the relationship between you and Miriam can be relaxed and warmed, if you take your daughter's special disposition—and nobody knows her the way you do—sufficiently into account, respect her deepest wishes, honor her strengths. So, how can demands or injunctions—born of warmth—take on more the character of "communications," or rather, how can they be brought to the child in such a way that she does not close herself off from the situation at hand, but is receptive instead? Which situations come in question here? I have given you a few recommendations and thought impulses in our conversation already. I have intended them as points of reference for you. What you need to clarify for yourself besides—and you need to be as self-critical about it as you can—is whether you really only tell her or forbid her to do something if you *have to*.[57]

~ 10 ~
What is the Status of a Teacher's Humility?

The quality of a pedagogical relationship depends little on what we do or refrain from externally. In this regard, the debate over education is based on premises that are far removed from reality. Parents, teachers and educators imagine themselves to be furnished with a god-like abundance of power, or at least they believe they deserve it. Thus they react with consternation and confusion and take it as a personal offense when it becomes clear just what little influence they really have.

We need to read writings and lectures on education carefully with this in mind. Even where the arguments are made with emphasized mildness and understanding, as a rule every line bears witness to the fact that the vassal status of children *as such* is a foregone conclusion; there are widely diverging conceptions of how vassals are to be treated, that's all. Dictatorially? With lenience? Can they be better controlled by means of open compulsion, or by giving them the feeling that they are doing voluntarily what they have to do anyway? Even love is recommended as an instrument of power, according to the motto of "positive reinforcement" (giving attention in order to win obedience). One sometimes gets the impression from books or lectures on pedagogy that the subject of discussion is a conquered people, and not those who carry knowledge of the future in the impulses of their wills. (This occasioned Werner Kuhfuss to remark that "the holiest and most taboo thing in the relationship between adults and children is the will of the children.") With so flagrantly inaccurate an assessment of the mandate of education, it is no wonder that everything fails. According to Kuhfuss, many experienced educators "react like deposed kings and queens" to the shrinkage of authority they are forced to accept and unable to explain. "Others . . . do not even make it as far as the throne. The subjects, the children, refuse to obey." They do so in order to make us understand what in the age of the consciousness soul we *have* to understand: "There is only one educator, and that is . . . the child in the person educating himself. Education is the art of providing the child in the human being with the opportunity to educate and raise himself."[58]

In the worst case, we can abuse or neglect a child; we can subject her to unceasing pedagogical overload to such extent that she resigns, outwardly submits. But there is one thing no one can ever do, and that is to manipulate what is the child's own, deepest, innermost sense. The *essential* is inaccessible to our sphere of influence. Of course, denial of this essential hampers its *emergence*. "Every tug or draw in the right direction is strengthening and confirming. Every pressure, even with the best of intentions, is weakening. Unfortunately, we are forced to recognize most education as pressure" (Kuhfuss). I have on various occasions characterized a "tug" or a "draw" as an *evocative* attitude toward education and upbringing, evocative meaning calling forth as opposed to calling in, pressuring, or manipulating. We are not even distantly the gods who are supposed to or able to make a child "into an orderly (or fully valid) human being." Rather we are allowed to take part in the completely different, amazing events that can liberate us quickly from the tendencies to dominate and rule, if we can permit them to become alive within us as grand pictures.

Before we even receive her as "a guest that is looking for the way" (Jirina Prekop / Christel Schweizer), the child raises upright her entelechy of hope to a place beyond the reach of our influence, to the *space of innocence*. She does so in the midst of a circle of higher beings, whose willing, feeling and thinking *are* what we human beings in our innermost are *seeking*: goodness, justice, truth. The unborn soul partakes in a grand future image of humanity, into which she wants to integrate her own individual motif. Nowadays this pre-conceptional process of raising oneself upright and imitating takes place in an unprecedented atmospheric nearness to *Christ*.[59] The child is being inspired by the *child of humanity* himself; in each birth the event of Bethlehem resounds. When the child resolves to entrust herself to us, she does so in agreement with those higher beings (one of them— her angel—is assigned to her as a "conscientious companion"), and is filled with the impression of her transition through the sphere of pure human love. Seen from "within," birth is this act of self-entrustment, which then touches all human beings selected by the child[60] to play a protecting, accompanying, comforting, healing role in her life (these four concepts will occupy us in chapter 11).

The angelic world is extending into our world; the nearness of the Christ is tangible; the configuration of time is pivoting (the future rather than the past is becoming the point of departure for events); we are being called on to receive and to carry on "the work of gods." When Rudolf Steiner put forth this concept in the introduction to his *Study of Man*, it was certainly not his intention to abet the pedagogical arrogance that confronts the child when speaking of the child as "a dough whose ingredients are stirred out of his inherited disposition, kneaded by the hand of the educator into the desired future, and baked done in the oven of time" (Elisabeth Lukas). To whom do we owe the privilege and/or the ability to do nothing less than continue *the work of gods*? The child. The idea of childhood has no foundation without the insight that it is not possible to influence the educational process unless the child empowers us to do so. The *child* is the divine messenger. Not the educator. The educator is given back a piece of his or her lost closeness to heaven by being given the chance to prove him- or herself worthy of this gift. The same holds true for the social organism as a whole, if one looks at it in the right way: there are no social configurations *that make sense*, unless *childhood* empowers us to make them. It is up to us to find ways to implement this empowerment.[61]

Suggestion for Artistic Implementation of Education and Child Rearing
        Start every day by deeply immersing yourself in this mental picture: when the child falls asleep, s/he returns to the place

from which s/he originally came to us with a great gesture of giving, of devotion, and of trust; this act of coming to us repeats itself every morning when the child awakens. In the evening of every ending day, I must strip the past of its power. I must literally watch all grudges that have accumulated melt away, everything in the way of habit and routine that has crept into my relationship with the child—all this I must watch melt away before the unprecedented event of warmth that consists in *the child giving itself to me again day after day.* Is not the durability of this trust striking, when I consider how often I lack patience and understanding? In order to really start over each day, we must find a new relationship to sleep, the "little brother of death."

When the child goes to sleep, the finished world really does die. As a parent or teacher, one can confirm this process, as it were; one can allow the relationship-healing force that lives within it to become active by consciously engaging in it, paying particular attention to those children with whom one has a challenging time. Here it is important to find essential concepts that encompass in a image the inner aspect of the event. At night, the child withdraws into *the space of innocence, the pure sphere of hope,* where what matters is not what was, but only what we wish out of the force of love. For my part I practice breaking with what has been and orienting myself entirely toward what is yet to come; I do so by ensuring my love for the child for the day and the time to come. Assuming I do this, and assuming that in sleep she hears what I am thinking and feeling, I place myself in a position to receive her the next day in such a way that I am a sounding board for what she brings along out of the night. With these prerequisites, starting over every day is a powerful technique for building trust. Regular, conscious exertion in all tranquility, best combined with planning something specific to do with or for the child the next day that stands out as an offer to form a relationship, leads to success. By success I mean not making the child more partial to my intentions and expectations, but only *deepening the relationship*. Nothing else.

⌒11⌒
Understanding Confirmation: Protecting, Accompanying, Comforting, Healing (the Axle)

But how do we do justice to the task the child himself has given us, if all our outer doings are so marginal? If we want to answer this question, we first have to clarify how the task is actually framed. The task is *to understand*. Active (sculptural) understanding means being ready for the nearest event of initiation. "Being touched and melted by becoming thou" (Martin Buber) heightens my attention. Thus heightened, my attention takes the child's future aspect (that is, the part of him that is surging to be realized as a form) and provides it with an anticipatory form in counter-space. We are responsible for the advent-like preparation for the coming day (and external things belong here as well, albeit marginally), for filling what is open (the future) with a mood of expectation, a mood that feels its way into the future. I do not mean *certain* or binding expectations or intentions, but rather an inner preparedness (and a bracing of oneself) for the events announced to us. Announced? I repeat: we have been initiated! The child comes from the fullness of the future into a world ruled by a dearth of forces of the past (to this alone we owe our experience of the present[62]) and entrusts his secret to us. But this secret is not given to us as knowledge in the sense of *mental pictures*, but rather as a *faculty* that comes to manifestation in a mood of heightened attentiveness that is the capacity to find the proper (acknowledging) attitude, gestures, tone of voice, language, and so forth, and to find them with certainty of feeling. The child can form himself into this productive mood of expectation; he recognizes himself in it. Our perceptive sense ("presence of mind") for educationally artistic situations establishes the child's connection with his angel. An "honoring atmosphere" is the content of our shaping; *value-discerning* (not *evaluating*) vision—the corresponding mood of soul—is the faculty by which the shaping is done. Whoever discovers education to be an art that takes place in a field of events, and whoever then begins consciously to move around in the field, will find that out of this attitude externals can be arranged with the humblest of means and entirely without exaggerated pedagogical zeal, and in a way that the child will nevertheless feel *acknowledged*. No circumstances can automatically guarantee this decisive quality, not even the most ideal ones, nor can even the strongest loyalty to principles of social hygiene. On the other hand the ideal *can* be achieved even under averse outer conditions.

Once more, then: what is education and upbringing— once the arrogance of feasibility falls away and one takes seriously the initiatory character of the educational relationship? I repeat four central concepts mentioned previously: protecting, accompanying, comforting, healing. These are basic techniques of education as an art (in the sense of "moral technique," the notion coined by Steiner). They work together when we comprehend creatively, and they pull the rug out from under any and every intention to manipulate pedagogically. Let us dwell on the individual concepts.

Protecting

In addition to the obvious protection against external dangers, we need to protect *the mystery*. The mystery has been entrusted to me, the chosen protector. Despite its fundamental indestructibility, the mystery needs my protection because it would be unable to unfold itself if it were exposed to the storm of the world. It would close itself off. The mystery is what "is yet to be brought forth [but what] itself generates the capacity to create itself." In this sphere in which time (or the relation between cause and effect) is inverted, the concept of action turns into its opposite. What we normally call activity (intentional, intervening movement directed toward something or someone) does *nothing* in the sphere of the mystery; rather, it turns back on itself and creates distance. All I perceive is mirror images of my own intentions. This interrupts the phenomenon *relationship*. By contrast, what in the object world is the exact opposite of action—that is, perception—is in the sphere of the mystery the activity proper that creates and that establishes relationships. What matters is not this or that content of perception, but rather the very power of perception, i.e., attention. Through it (or rather *into* it), the mystery can unfold itself. The capacity to be attentive in this sense comes to me from the mystery itself. The finished product requires my (co)creative comprehension to be able to give rise to itself, and I am drawn into the process in such a way that what will be arriving out of the future already lives in my mood of reception. In the sphere of the mystery, this listening, whose nature it is to probe the future with its feeling, is the protecting activity proper. I shield the mystery in this way. The child needs for its self-empowerment my listening acknowledgement of its possibility, my initiated sensing of the future. The attainment of this clairvoyance of feeling is not a kind of hocus-pocus. All it takes is deep devotion, "reverence for the minute [small]" (Steiner, GA 317), and tranquility. One must inwardly come to rest and learn to maintain silence. Noise and talkativeness are off the mark. What are noise and talkativeness in the sphere of the mystery? Evaluating, judging, drawing conclusions, pursuing intentions. One need not so much as open one's mouth to be constantly talking at the child. The following attitude is decisive: am I practicing restraint in *judging*? Am I capable of *astonishment*?

Accompanying

Besides the self-understood helping companionship through the foreignness of external life, what matters is that we *allow time* for the mystery to unfold. Moreover, inner accompaniment demands that we avoid intentional intervention. We must stand at the child's side with a waiting attitude, simply be there, patient. While the protective gesture of attentively probing the future with one's feeling is an action of the moment, reserved for select hours and constantly threatened by outside distraction, the gesture of accompanying adds a quality that ensures constancy: *faithfulness*, persevering trust. Here as well, apparent inactivity is the actual creative activity. I bridle my advent-like expectation of an impending "miracle" and turn in sympathy to meet a process of *becoming*. The process as such awakens my interest; expectation matures into the ability to wait. The enemy here is impatience. The adult has broken the habit of talkativeness (the urge constantly to judge and to evaluate) and now stands before the task of practicing patience. In the sphere of the mystery, to accompany means to be able to wait—not in boredom, though, but rather in a participatory way. One must become attentive to the fact that initiated probing of the future, if it succeeds, bears a danger within: one is so near the mystery with one's sensation that one is tempted (but not entitled) to tear down the veil so that one can "make for oneself a clear picture." This is why just those mothers or fathers who are anxious of the future because of their deep understanding often tend to manipulate their children, out of the noblest of intentions. It is *impossible* to tear down the veil. What they consider unveiling is a pseudo-imagination or, as the case may be, a projection, in which the parents take their favorite notions and presumptions and combine them with elements of "genuine" vision to form a picture. Based on their feeling of advent, they confuse this artifice with genuine inner vision. True interest, which patiently waits and follows the process, provides protection from errors of this kind. The object of my attention needs to be the process of the child's development, not its result.

Comforting

Besides the obvious comforting attention for everyday sorrows, illness, injury, and so on, we need to meet setbacks and confusion that occur as the mystery unfolds, and in such a way that we dampen them and limit their effect. A child's greatest sorrow and deepest anxieties are released when her entelechy of hope is darkened. This happens through everything she experiences in the way of disrespect or rejection of her *pure will*. Adults who are moved by *motives foreign to the relationship* mislead the child by imposing expectations, demands, or restrictions on this pure will, or by otherwise encroaching on it (prejudices are also encroachments). This amounts to disrespect and/or neglect. The entelechy of hope is also darkened when the child encounters negative attitudes and modes of action, such as hostility, plotting and scheming, pitilessness, injustice, and deceit. One can tell a child has been abused by motives that have nothing to do with the relationship when, for instance, she develops a failure anxiety; one sees in a strange and seemingly reasonless abashedness that she is dismayed over "evil." Failure anxiety and shame can clothe themselves in widely diverging forms of "abnormal behavior," depending on the particular nature of the child, but the basic characteristic is always a deep distress of some kind. Experiences of such darkening of the child's entelechy of hope are unavoidable. But we can comfort her in the face of them by calling her out of her distress by the authority vested in us by child herself. By *"calling her out"* I mean addressing her as "thou." Of course, we need to see here the concept of effectiveness and/or action in a new light. We normally consider the *answer* to be active, rather than the question. To ask a question means to describe the arena of action more or less precisely, while to give an answer means to create facts. But when we want to comfort a child in distress, the inverse holds. Teachings or explanations (answers) are of little comfort. In the sphere of the mystery they act as repellants. By contrast, there is a comforting show of trust in the art (!) of asking questions in the manner of the initiate. The key question, asked in confidence, is the address, "thou." In a higher sense, it is also the answer. The one asking the question "knows" the mystery better than its own bearer, who has initiated and selected him or her (the asker of the question) as the guardian of her mystery. Of course, the "knowing" here does not involve mental pictures; rather, it is an intuitive "acquaintance," the described mood of receptivity that feels out the future (c.f. part 1, chapter 5) and turns into the gesture of questioning. I must step before the child fervently questioning and filled with wishes, so that my attitude signals to him: you give me a gift when you contemplate yourself. I must with my entire person—"touched and melted by becoming thou"—*be* the question: Who are you? This is comforting! When I find this attitude, the angel of the child puts the right (utterable) questions into my mouth, and the essential one that needs no uttering the angel puts into my gaze, my fingertips, my body language, the sound of my voice, the question that is not interested in finding out this or that, but that is aimed at and envelops the very entity "thou" that is confirmation in its very essence. I can teach a child about time past and about the finished world, to be sure, but not about what is to come. With respect to what is to come, I am the one who is learning, the one who is being heaped with gifts, and I am only giving back out of the plenty I have received, when the child stands before me in need of comfort and consolation, that is, in need of remembering. The first basic principle is: Motives distant from the relationship (pedagogical intentions that have not been won through listening into the child herself) create anxiety and distress to the point of resignation, and the experience of lovelessness, whether meted out to the child directly or only witnessed among fellow men by her, causes shame to the point of intimidation or, as the case may be, to the point that the pain of shame causes defensive withdrawal behavior. (Resignation and shame can also occur with the "killjoy effect"; then you have the notorious little mischief maker, who really only lacks consolation, and now on top of everything else is supposed to be disciplined by means of hectic and anti-relational procedures.) The second basic principle is: Whenever possible one should spare the child both experiences, but it is impossible to spare her *all* of them. The third basic principle is: The key question to the thou itself, cultivated in the spirit of a soul exercise and directed at the sphere of the mystery as a reminding call, reveals the power of consolation and helps a hundred times more than any outer measure.

Healing

Protecting attentiveness (listening), accompanying interest (waiting), and comforting trust (asking) are the qualities that work together in the educative faculty of understanding confirmation. They cannot be separated in reality, but they can be separated for the sake of observation, just as one can observe a tree from different angles. It gives a different picture from each angle, and yet one knows it is one and the same tree. We need to learn to look at spiritual-soul connections from different angles in just as differentiated a fashion as if we were walking around a tree in physical space. This is where spirituality begins in a concrete sense. The tree that we are walking around in the present example is the concept of understanding confirmation (or creative comprehension). This concept characterizes an inner attitude that must flow into everything we do and do not if we are to succeed in making the quantum leap from education to education as an art. We can also describe this quantum leap as the advance from regimented to healing education, if we bear in mind that regimentation is any influence from *without*, while healing is the *inner* shaping of a relationship based on the idea of childhood. But the aspects of the basic attitude of healing mentioned up to now need to be supplemented. The connecting element, the linking piece, is missing. Attentiveness, interest and trust unfold their healing (one might also say blessing) force only if and when in the sphere of the mystery *the child meets the child*. And thus we come to the core of the idea of childhood. The actual aid to destiny, that is, healing accompaniment of the process of incarnation itself happens whenever the inner child of the chosen companion reveals itself to the one who is the child in body. Initiation is based on mutuality; it is an act of agreement at the threshold. I seal the pact by (re)tracing my mystery and taking the child into my trust. Here too we speak of an inner activity. The person who remembers that s/he is designed after the Human Being, who seeks to connect with the creative source, who finds his or her way back (or, as the case may be, forward) to the entelechy of hope, to the "inner child" who stands there grand, bright, and unscathed, where beginning and end fall together, that person escapes what we have called the threefold loss of creativity,[63] and really can protect, accompany, and comfort a child and, all in all, educate her through healing.

By now it should be clear from the established context that by "healing" I mean not "elimination of a state of illness," but rather "guidance to the essential," i.e., "salvation" (Steiner) from the illnesses of the times. I am speaking of the posture of curative education described previously. Places where the educational relationship is cultivated must be permeated with artistic spirit: laboratories of the future, nurseries of human hope. Consolation is the key gesture directed toward the child, in which the child recognizes himself in the face of the darkening of his hope. Supportive companionship is accompaniment of the child with interest and patient expectation. Listening attentiveness provides protection. Healing encompasses all of this and yet is more. Healing means giving hope, to give hope means to *have* hope, and whether or not a person has hope is a question of thinking. A person's hopeful thinking about a person is *loving* thinking, that is, thinking inspired by the essence of childhood. Thus, the circle closes: institutions that do justice to childhood are only possible out of thinking that is permeated by the warmth force of childhood. If we perceive the nearness of Christ (the child of humanity) in the sphere of the spirit that borders directly on this world, the angelic realm, and if we take up what emanates from

Him and recast it into concepts of artistic education, a warmer time can begin for "difficult" children, which will spread to *all* children, and from there will be passed on to the entire social life. The utopia of a new Christendom— free of dogma, demands for power, and hypocrisy—is initially a pedagogical task. The adjective "dfficult" is more accurately applied to those unwilling to cease plodding along the convenient and well-trodden path.

∽12∽
The Child in the Context of the World

Every educator has heard at one time or another that education is in its essence a relationship or, more precisely, the child woven into a complex fabric of relationships. He is woven into this fabric as a thinking entity, a feeling entity, and a willing entity. On all three levels, he participates concretely in what happens nearer to or further away from him. I am not saying that the child is defenseless, exposed to events (that is a pious fairy tale) but that he takes part in them. We need to take this fact seriously enough. We should rid ourselves of the custom of constantly staring at the difficult child with the intention of finding a comfortably understandable and monocausal justifying context (disquieting experiences in the past, errors in upbringing, physiological malfunctions of the brain, or other dysfunctions) for his failures, his restlessness, anxiety, or sadness. We need to practice—and this is not easy—vision of the entire context or, in other words, of the world context as the respective child experiences it. This presupposes that we feel our way into the child. The world context is the most personal pre-conceptual interpretation of the world, the prioritization and evaluation of things, events, or customs by feeling. What seems minute to me can be gigantic to the child, and vice versa. Many children react with a hypersensitivity, even allergy, to certain impressions or situations that in our estimation are unremarkable. It is conceiveable that karmic influences are at play in such situations, which individualize the child's experience of the world and thus lead over- or underemphasis.[64] In the course of a child's youth, this strongly individual character of *perception* changes into individualized *motivation* and *expressive power*, while on the level of perception, for the most part (but never completely), it arranges itself with the customary, with consensus. The transformation continues in the course of the person's individual striving for knowledge (assuming it actually sets in). There are children who cannot bear a mood of fundamental change or of bidding farewell even in the slightest dosages. Others feel deeply insecure at dawn or dusk, or in situations that have, even indirectly, the character of dawn or dusk: minor (in the musical sense) moods, the gradual coming to rest of a dynamic occurrence, a sound dying out or, conversely, the first intonation of music, or of any new situation that would evoke the sense of being in between. Still others have difficulty dealing with the notion of leaving something open, or with having to wait. I once knew a little boy who felt the wind to be threatening because he could feel it but not see it; and everything else in the context of his world that had the indirect quality of windiness (anything in motion that could not be taken hold of, anything light, sanguine, whirling, springy) made him beside himself. On occasion, I encounter children decried as "poor in soul," who always cause a disturbance in mood-rich situations, rather than being deeply touched and filled with astonished devotion, as is expected. It becomes evident after a brief, unprejudiced acquaintance that these children are by no means "poor in soul," but on the contrary are so receptive for heartfelt moods that the adults with the callouses on their own souls simply have no idea of it. These children sense impressions as unbearably strong that for everybody else address the life of feeling in a marginal way.

One must be attentive to phenomena of this kind. Moreover, anyone unwilling to remain stuck in externals can acquire a perceptive faculty for the plane of body-free communication, that is, of encounters not bound to (mis)communication in the physical-spatial. General ignorance pertaining to the extrasensory dimension of the relational fabric is rampant. One should not believe for an instant that it is of no consequence what the adult thinks about a child, how the adult feels about the child *between* their face to face meetings, or is what the adult's mood toward the child as s/he falls asleep in expectation of meeting the next day. One should not underestimate with what a darkening (or brightening) effect the "deeds" of a third party, who need not even be physically present, can creep into a person's effort to come to terms with a child. Sometimes it can cause a miracle if someone is taken into confidence who more *inwardly* than outwardly accompanies the child with genuine understanding and warm-hearted interest. In other instances, it takes a gutsy resolution on the part of the parents to no longer admit the opinion of a negatively-attuned observer or collaborator, that is, to ignore his advice and cast his catastrophe-predicting prognosis to the wind, or perhaps even to see to it that this person disappears from the group of people who have a say in the matter.

The things and people in the vicinity of the child are enmeshed with each other to form a living context of events, into which the child is integrated in a much subtler way than one generally imagines. We need to *practice* directing our attention to this fact. When a circle of people forms around a so-called difficult child who consider it their task, in a joint effort toward understanding, to create a supportive and *protective* spiritual space, there emanates from this group of people a direct healing effect. For in this way an "inner sector," or tranquility and essentiality, is set apart from the complex fabric of events, in which the child (in the so-called mental level) can find shelter whenever it feels confused and lonesome. Of course, such an "inner sector" cannot replace direct physical closeness, but it most certainly can supplement it. And it is a very significant supplement. Finally, in order to complete the picture, *world events* as a whole also need to be taken into account, that is, the societal circumstances, the states of the earth and of humankind. We can assume that every child achieves during sleep (!) an awareness that it is universally included and that it participates in the drama of the *destiny of humanity*. The child takes part in this destiny, and it does so in a very certain way; it is entirely out of the child's own super-temporal entelechy of hope that s/he looks upon the events of the world and recognizes for what they are the hope-destroying forces at work there, and s/he feels inwardly threatened. Here, also, much depends on our attitude: has my point of reference to the *human being* become a source of educational inspiration? Upon awakening and immersing into her everyday situation, does the child experience that people are there in whom hope for humanity lives, and that in this regard we are her *companions*?

Excerpt from a Conversation:
Robert L., five years old, is discussed during visiting hours on account of his excessively spiteful behavior.[65]

PARENTS: He believes we are constantly putting him under pressure out of pure malice. But we only put on pressure when it is really necessary.

COUNSELOR: How have you come to this conclusion?

PARENTS: He frequently says, "You are always, always so mean!" And when he says that he has tears of rage in his eyes.

COUNSELOR: And from that you conclude that he thinks you are acting out of pure malice?

PARENTS: He considers it intentional cruelty. Where in the world does this mistrust come from? When I say, "Comb your hair," he starts heaping reproach on me.

COUNSELOR: What kind of reproach is that?

PARENTS: Well, he shouts, "But I don't want to comb hair! You're mean! You're always bothering me! I want to play! Mean Daddy!"

COUNSELOR: But you can't interpret these words literally when they're coming from a five-year-old.

PARENTS: I don't know. . .

Counselor: I wonder if he really is accusing you of malice and intentional cruelty. I can't imagine that.

PARENTS: Then why is he constantly resisting? Why this blaming?

COUNSELOR: I don't know that yet. But if you feel offended because you believe your boy is accusing you of bad intentions, and if the only reason you feel that way is that he is hurling rude and rascally slander at you the moment he doesn't like something, then you are bringing an allegation into play that can't be easily deduced just from recalcitrant behavior. A pure presumption, and a rather distrustful one at that, don't you think? Couldn't it be that the *recalcitrance problem* is Robert's, and that the problem with mistrust is *yours*? Let's assume that a child has really sensitive skin and that after his bath he screams, "Ow! You're hurting me! Mean Mommy! Mean Daddy!" It would be wrong, wouldn't it, to conclude, "My child believes I'm maliciously trying to hurt him." The drying off just hurts, that's all. What hurts is "mean."

PARENTS: So you believe we mistrust our child?

COUNSELOR: Not quite. I much rather wonder if you aren't burdening your already difficult relationship with Robert even more by tending to sense some things as personal affronts that are not at all directed at you. This often leads to misunderstandings in partnerships, in love relationships, in work relationships, and in teacher-student relationships, just as it does between parents and their children. I might even go so far as to say that you have made incredible efforts with Robert, and that you are reading his recalcitrance as ingratitude. You feel unfairly judged by him and not sufficiently acknowledged. Please don't take that as criticism. There is no question but that you are good parents. But we as adults are not allowed any claim to acknowledgement of our efforts by our children. We have been more than acknowledged by being given a child at all. We owe thanks for that to the child and to heaven. You need to be aware of what a privilege it is that you have been chosen by Robert as parents. It is important for us to be on guard against impulses of feeling offended or insulted; these always have something to do with a false estimation of one's own role. Children are not obligated in everything to share our view of what is good for them. And when you consider that they have to prepare for a whole long life, you will understand that they can only take our wishes and sensitivities into account to a limited extent.

There follows a conversation about what the counselor has just said. The parents cannot immediately understand in what respect they are privileged, but the thought interests them.

Parents: Maybe we're too sensitive, that could be. But Robert's obstinacy quite obviously *is* directed against us. What else could it be? He simply has no sense for the fact that we want what is best for him.

Counselor: That is *your* belief. He spoke very lovingly about you to me. I have the impression that he has blind faith in you. He admires his father like a great hero. No other man competes with him. And you, Mrs. L., are his refuge. His comforter and healer. From you comes everything that is nice and pleasant. You always know what to do when he feels weak and sick.

Parents: But why?

Counselor: It is quite possible that a child senses the love of his parents, or even presupposes them like a phenomenon of nature, and *in spite of that* lives under the impression that he always has to defend himself. And besides, he also resists in kindergarten. And with Grandma. At some point you need lay to rest all your presumptions, your disappointments and feelings of having been insulted, and start making exact observations. When does he resist? When does he *not* resist? How does he behave then? All I ever hear is that Robert is obstinate, he scolds and screams. The scolding and screaming is not the entire boy! Yesterday I saw the wonderful imagination he has when he builds a landscape, and what delightful and colorful stories come to him then. Moreover, I am impressed at the fundamentally positive way he speaks about everyone. That shows a lot of primal trust and benevolence. Robert doesn't seem to consider the "scenes" that are always happening in kindergarten and at home all that tragic. In his naïvete he considers adults to be much too great and powerful for him to make them any serious problems. He is actually a sunny and carefree little guy, and we mustn't deprive him of his joy for life by reducing him to a bratty nuisance.

PARENTS: We see it that way, too, when you get right down to it. . . But then there's always this friction, the complaints from the kindergarten, the comments from relatives and friends. . .

COUNSELOR: Turn a deaf ear on any and all "comments" in which you don't also hear affinity for or acknowledgement of Robert! If you *do* hear them, you can accept even critical advice. But only then. Above all, infinitely much depends on *your* maintaining —unconditional—appreciation for your boy. He is entitled to your considering every *beautiful* side of his nature at least three times as important as any of his "difficult" aspects. And we still haven't clarified just what is "difficult." A lot of nice things come out in ways that make very peculiar and mussed up first impressions. Always remember that most babies look like withered fruit just after they are born and are incapable of anything but screaming, wriggling and sleeping. That is an archetypal picture. And that is just the way it is with incipient human capacities and characteristics. People are right when they say that in general the only ones who think a newborn baby is beautiful are the baby's parents. The look of love sees more, and more deeply.

What it really sees is what belongs to the future. *This* is the look we need to direct toward a child's "difficult behavior." Regardless of what others say.

PARENTS: Yes, that probably is what really matters. And you are sure that our assumption is unfounded? Robert does not distrust us?

COUNSELOR: I am absolutely sure of it. We must start down a path of understanding for a while. Robert has "reasons" for his behavior which, for the moment, are beyond our grasp. That needs to change. As long as we don't learn to sense his hidden motives, we can't do anything. But to start with, the myth needs to be done away with that he has a negative, hostile relation to you two. That is not the case! With this allegation you only burden him and yourselves.

PARENTS: Where might this constant bristling come from, then?

COUNSELOR: I have a very tense relationship with suspicions, and especially with psychological diagnoses that are based on them. For this reason, and because I don't know Robert well yet, I'm going to answer you indirectly and with great reservation: there have been few occasions in my life that have caused me to fret more than occasions where I have had to reject well-meant and genuinely reasonable advice from people who were sincerely worried about me. This voice inside me would say, and quite authoritatively, "No!" Haven't you ever had that? You somehow have the feeling that you need to protect yourself against the very act of being influenced. Sometimes it only shows years later that that feeling was right. You might have sustained a few bruises over not having followed the good advice, but that was the price to be paid for an unprecedented achievement or meeting that would not have been possible without the "thorny path." Now, for the sake of fairness to Robert, we have to grant the possibility that this situation might apply to him. Experience shows that it is pertinent to many children's biographies. "Difficult children," whom a few people, mainly the parents, have conspired to champion (not in a pampering or uncritical way, but with trust and esteem), oftentimes go amazing ways, and then we say in retrospect: Ouch! That child might have ended up in the psychotherapeutic or remedial mill! That child just missed being subjected to all kinds of repair actions or being put out of action entirely, because the abilities we see now proclaimed themselves in the way all "ability infants" do: asleep, in general, but otherwise screaming, wriggling around, shriveled, shapeless. . . .[66] All we know for now is that Robert has a deep aversion toward being influenced and having to integrate himself. Let's leave it at that, for the time being. He has a bigger problem than many other children; there needn't be any hidden cause behind it. That is not to say that Robert's problem is *acquired*. The matter could also just have to do with expectations for the future, with a presentiment for what is to come. What the situation demands for the moment is what I would call the posture of creative non-knowing, listening, questioning. And abstaining from any and all suspicions. Even if we were to do nothing else, that will bring us forward.

≈ 13 ≈
The Pathology of Life Mastered and the Power of Astonishment

Is it reasonable that a child's unmanageable or divergent behavior be assessed as a sign of individual failure in a time when interpersonal relations (conversational and love relationships, legal, work, and economic relations) on all levels are profoundly disturbed? When speaking of social circumstances, one often forgets that circumstances are primarily *relationships*, and only secondarily material existence, economic conditions, and so forth. Disturbed relations for their part stand in mutual relationship with disturbances in the *awareness* of relationships. The consciousness that is counterinspired out of the force field of cold sets relationship standards and generates relational structures within which only this counterinspired consciousness can provide any orientation: objectification (thinking), mechanization (feeling), and instrumentalization (willing) of the interhuman fabric. This sets a machinery in motion that lames socio-sculptural productivity and is unable to come to rest *of its own accord*. Truly, the *only* possibility to realize Beuys's "warmth/time machine"[67] is through the influx from sources that are not layered over by the counterinspired system. Thus, interpenetration from the sphere of the still and always, impact the presence of the Human Being (from the "sphere of innocence"). Beuys's conceptional design to counter the cold machine, whose expressive force lies precisely in its logical impossibility—a machine in the current sense cannot be a structure that produces its own warmth and time—refers to the *transformation* of the principle of the machine. Thus, it is not a matter of mechanics, but rather a reason-filled and creative construction of relationships. This is the meaning of socio-sculptural productivity.

Children come toward us from out the sphere of innocence. *We come toward ourselves* from this same sphere, if and when we allow the event of artistic education to occur and thus become understanding allies of those children who cause *chaos* in the cold machine. Such chaos always has something to do with the fact that warmth/motion events disturb the undercooled uniformity, thus causing incalculable, *formable,* situations (free spaces for action) to occur. To recognize these and to use them with presence of mind is the unuttered plea of special children to us, and it is no accident that this plea is becoming evermore urgent. To assume the defectivist standpoint is to ignore or refuse this plea. Condemnation of these children as "deficient," and so on, their "need for special care" (Steiner) with weakness in adapting to the laws of the cold machine *always* happens according to criteria and under the spell of the cold machine itself. Sometimes this is unavoidable, but we must not deceive ourselves.

In our hearts we neglect education as an institution (and by that I mean not only the political and administrative level, but also the configuration of thoughts, feelings and relationships in which we all have a part); hence we neglect its very core. Does this *not compel* childhood to put up resistance? And does this resistance not have to come out of the center of warmth and movement, that is, out of the heart and will? The same place where the neglect takes place?

By "childhood" I mean a supersensible field that shelters and connects all children up to a certain age. In this field "resolutions" are made by all means, and these resolutions come from a wisdom that stands head and shoulders above our highly esteemed rational understanding. We as adults are connected to this field to the extent that we make ourselves acquainted with the entity of childhood in the way described. The driving force of the cold machine is a mixture of fear, envy, power hunger, vanity, and materialistic obsessions. This fuel has been analyzed frequently and impressively. The impelling force of the warmth/ time machine, though, is withdrawn from the conventional analytic grip. It is that substance of hope that streams into the process of incarnation: the essential nature of childhood, that through thinking can be grasped as the *idea* of childhood. In this connection, it is worth a person's while to have a look at the fact that the so-called childhood behavioral disorders, which cause us so much puzzlement, *are* not only turbulences across the board in the warmth/relationship sector and the time/movement sector, but that they *cause* these turbulences, which means that they hit us right where our own fears and insecurities lie and where we ourselves have withdrawn into the deceptive securities of the cold machine.[68]

Whenever one wants to draw attention to these matters, one is dashed against the defense bulwark of a collective self-deception that is becoming ever denser. This self-deception pre-supposes the average neurotic relationship to the world as the reasonable measure of things. A self-critical and culturally-critical examination of the *pathology of life mastered* in times of spiritual superficiality and social frigidity—the one presupposes the other—occurs only at the very edge. This examination is also urgently necessary in connection with the question of education. The fact that so-called difficult children may be wanting to defend a patch of health of the soul against the psycho-pathological consensus, and thereby not only become conspicuous and cause disturbances but also fail (caused by us!) in alarmingly many cases, is a notion with which we *seriously* need to acquaint ourselves in order to find our way out of this pedagogical dead end. One chief reason for the failure of the healthy impulses that want to become active through such children, as well as for their deviation into resignation, fear, or destructiveness, is the tacit agreement on the part of the adult world (from the grass roots of a helpless, resigned parenthood up to the academic "elite" and pediatric specialists), to pathologize everything that exposes and wants to shatter the pathology of the times, pathologize in two senses of the word: to declare sick and to drive into sickness. It is not the special children who are the problem; rather it is the fact that we see them in a contorted way in the mirror of our damaged conception of the world. This contorted perception has an *effect*: the children do not recognize themselves in us and hence react disconcertedly and with agitation, while we further assess their disconcerted and agitated reactions as the confirmation of our contortions. It is up to us to break the vicious circle. The attitude that can enable us to break the circle can be expressed with the words Lao-tse uses about true knowledge: "I stand still, calmly and wishlessly like a newborn, like a person without a home."

We have become acquainted with the qualities of protecting, accompanying, comforting, and healing, which comprehends and goes beyond the first three. These are fundamental attitudes of education and upbringing as an art that we need to practice. In the mystery sector of "protection" our *listening attentiveness* is located; the prerequisite for accompaniment of the child's destiny is *patient waiting*; comforting consolation lies in learning in a deeper sense—by reminding the child, as it were—to *ask*; and the proper force of healing (making whole) is the *event of hope*, through which, for the educational relationship as well, the precept bears itself out: When two of you come together in *my* name, *I* am there in your midst. These four qualities are reflected in the thought from Lao-tse quoted above: hearing transformed into something higher; empathy transformed into something higher because it has a say in the matter, but also because it waits patiently; comprehension transformed into something higher through being a pure question; and the power of hope, which condenses all this into the healing atmosphere and which streams in out of the future.[69] These steps can now be reformulated into simple indications for contemplation and self-examination.

Still:

The many eager voices inside me that comment on everything before I have properly perceived it, be now silent. I have no personal opinions and do not know what this or that means. My consciousness is an empty room, in which the melody of your life may now resound. I listen.

Tranquil:

My fears and sensitivities are not what matters! I do not want to avoid anything; neither do I want to follow any intentions, save the one: to understand you. No matter what happens, I welcome it. My attention knows no preferences. I wait.

Wishless:

My wish for you and our present relationship to correspond to my needs is of no occasion; where there is no wish, there is no disappointment. I am entitled to nothing. My only demand is to recognize your demands and to do justice to them. I ask.

Homeless:

Conventional expectations, acquired measures, social prejudices must not influence me. The future know no customs, the status quo lies always behind me. I step out into the open and seek you. I hope.

Hope here means not the hope for a particular thing for oneself, but rather a fundamental attitude, in this case one toward the child that one could call a feeling of advent. In the mood of homelessness, the ability to wait (dis-interested) that distinguishes tranquility is heightened to one of joyful expectation of what is coming, of what is being announced. Hope in the proper sense is the preparedness or readiness to be surprised or found in a state of astonishment. For this reason, hope is clouded by everything that I *presuppose* or make into a condition, or that I consider to be opportune, and so forth. People who are poor in hope are tied to the stake of stability, imprisoned in conventions, weighed down by the ballast of the unalterable and the habitual.

Listening, waiting, asking, hoping are the four gestures of the soul that are united in *astonishment*, four aspects of what we, along with Morgenstern, call "creative comprehending." The ability to listen presupposes quiet. The ability to wait presupposes tranquility. The ability to ask presupposes wishlessness. Hope awakens in the mood of homelessness.

The path of exercise indicated here leads to a true *art* of education, in which it is not a matter of instruction and behavioral architecture, but rather of finding an attitude toward children that renders calculated "measures" superfluous, because it enables intuitive action and it teaches *astonishment*.

⁓14⁓
Seeds of Ability: The Poetic Path

If one approaches the child with the question of their innate talents (their seeds of ability), an effort should be made toward recognizing spiritual justice. With this term we mean the attitude of esteem of which Martin Buber wrote that "measure and comparison have disappeared. It is up to you how much of the infinite becomes reality." Our question is aimed at the sphere of the mystery, at the *individual*. "Reverence and awe for the mysterious path of the child must be the beginning of the posture with which the educator approaches his task" (Steiner, GA 305; likewise all the following quotes in this chapter). One ought not to "pour something into" the child, but rather "have awe and reverence toward its spirit." He follows with the lapidary sentences whose weight is seldom acknowledged even among adherents to Waldorf education: "You cannot develop this spirit, it develops itself." This is why "the very greatest self-renunciation" on the part of the educator is the most effective force of education as an art. Obviously, no one is expected to renounce himself across the board all day long in a grumpy attitude of self sacrifice. Steiner means the opposite. Anyone who neglects the development of his own personality will not be able to find a relationship of trust with the child. But such a relationship is the only thing possible in the infinity of mutual hope. That is where the adult dedicates him or herself not only to the child bodily entrusted to him, but also to the *essence of childhood*, which the educator himself *is*. Steiner speaks of the "greatest possible self denial" of the self-interest that crowds its way into the pure wish to understand.

Self-interest is a motivation foreign to the relationship. Instead of pursuing any plans or intentions, we must "live in the environment of the child in a way that the child's spirit can develop its own life in sympathy through the mere presence of the life of the educator. What is in the educator himself ought not to live on (in the child) under compulsion." By means of this attitude of esteem (and that means an attitude of healing!), says Steiner, we alleviate *obstacles* to self development "in the physical and even a bit in soul existence."

Why in the physical, in particular? Because the child's body, which is still incredibly formable right down into the finest functional processes, can only become a *pliable instrument* of the spirit (which in itself cannot be influenced) if the child has the open space, formed out of our listening, waiting, questioning and hopeful empathy, to *move freely*. In this element of freedom, the sculptural forming ability of the I imprints impulses of destiny into the body as potential abilities that are *superior* to the influences of the environment and biologically inherited predispositions alike. The obstacles we are to eliminate through our heightened power of understanding, rather than piling up additional ones through *intentional educating*, are themselves the environmental and hereditary factors in the broadest sense of the word. These *overalienate* the entelechy of hope from two sides, endogenously (heredity), and exogenously (forced learning, pouring in). Thus Steiner was able to formulate the following as the "three golden rules" of the art of education:

> 1) *gratitude,* heightened to the status of a religious mood, toward what we receive through the child (we called it "initiation");
> 2) an awe-filled awareness for the fact "that the child depicts a divine *riddle*" (emphasis H.K.) which "the art of education is supposed to solve" (we spoke of the "sphere of the mystery," in which our *understanding* becomes a healing *deed*); and
> 3) a "method of educating practiced in love, through which the child educates himself instinctively through our presence, so that one does not endanger (his) freedom, which must be respected even where it is the unconscious element of the force of organic growth" (the *hope* aspect in its deeper significance).

What is decisive, then, is neither what *I* consider important nor what *society* considers important, but rather what the *child* does or takes up with particular devotion. We must take into account, though, that for children the proper thing almost always emerges in unforced, playful situations. Therefore, one only does justice to them if one pays attention to how they behave in the space in which they are free of expectations and demands. This space can be *created*. We create it by means of the heightened attentiveness described in chapter 11 (protecting). The child is most likely to reveal himself when he is alone with an adult in whose presence he feels totally relaxed. If the adult's attention is pure, unintentional, and unclouded by any ulterior motives, the child feels safe as if under a kind of protective shield, more so than in kindergarten or at school, while at unsupervised play with friends, even more than when he is playing by himself. Under this shield he can develop a mode of play that is unabashed and at the same time exclusive (as it were for the trusted spectator) and unintentionally aimed at the creation of beauty. Children show themselves with complete and utter candor in such situations. But it is not at all that simple to be a quiet audience, without seeming pushy and confusing the child. What counts here is inner reserve. I must not permit any thoughts or feelings of praise or rebuke to come up inside me; I must not be curious, must not have the intention of forming any conclusions from what I am witnessing. I must avoid inner intervention just as carefully as I do outer. One can listen to the child's play, or one can stalk it, and that makes the big difference. The view that *evaluates* or *assesses* intervenes inwardly, but so does the one that stares in undistanced delight; as does the artificial mannerism "I am God's gift to children." Likewise is irony, the self-indulging eye of the expert, mildly alienated but patronizing. I do not need to go on about grownups' rude behavior while they are watching children at play. They have this tendency on account of the illusion that they are superior. By contrast, the unpretentious attention that can be practiced can be compared to the mood

that lives in many Japanese haikus.[70] "The water of spring /
Comes slowly / From the mountains" (Buson). One may doubt
that a simple depiction of fact amounts to poetry; one might feel
the wish for adjectival embellishment and metaphoric garlands.
What we tend not to bear in mind is that one can hardly honor a
phenomenon more than by simply declaring its presence an artistic event. Artistically distinguishing the water of spring slowly
coming down from the mountains imparts it higher meaning
than it had before, precisely *because* the poet was not under the
impression that he had to improve, add, or explain anything.
Buson's statement is "'heavens, how blind I was. Only now do I
understand: The water of spring / Comes slowly / From the
mountains." "Nothing else is present than this one thing, but
this one thing cosmically" (Buber). Every word is a key to the
mystery of the picture, which for its part brings news of the invisible workshop in which pictures of this kind come about and
are put together to form the world as an entirety. Spring. Water.
Slowly. Come. Mountains. From there. . . . The poetic experience of the picture and of its elements is at the same time a new
creation. The person experiencing it is taking part in the creation
of the world.[71]

When we assume *this* attitude more and more, we give
the child the freedom to take hold of his body, to find his individual warmth/time body, movement body, expressive body.
One can practice observing in haiku fashion, by making it a rule
that one make diary entries in the style of poetic miniatures about
the child's behavior during play. In this way, one becomes accustomed to the kind of listening (rather than judgmental and

unintentional) participation through which an atmosphere can arise in which the child can *breathe freely* and *come to himself*. Basic rules for such diary entries, on which one then can meditate, are: no evaluations or opinions, not even coded ones; no verbal eruptions of feeling; no metaphors or allegories; a few and merely characterizing adjectives.

> The animals are sleeping
> Now she is rubbing the piece of flint gently
> On her cheek and humming a dark tone.

Animals. Flint. Cheek. Dark tone. Sleep. Rubbing. Humming. Gently. Call the scene forth before your inner eye again and again. Feel every word through every detail. The *child* is the creator of this complex of events, which, the longer I concentrate on it, the greater, more meaningful, downright sublime an effect it has on me, even if I am unable to say why this is so. The thought becomes a strong experience; through my quiet presence *I* have created the space in which this scene could run its course. It is not coincidence that I was present. Something happened *between us*. One will then make a remarkable discovery: while in the beginning one senses the cosmic nature of the scene ever more clearly and enters into the mood that one has just participated in a sacred event, this impression disappears after a time, leaving room for the quite confusing feeling that the entire event and its individual elements mean *nothing*. Something absurd creeps in. The memory picture collapses as it were out of the pinnacle of its dignity and beauty and leaves behind a vacuum. But if you listen into this vacuum rather than allowing other thoughts and feelings to stream in (which would be the more obvious thing to do), you will find that, inasmuch as it is a "vacuum," it no longer means anything in the customary sense. But at the same time the feeling arises out of the meaninglessness that we can circumscribe as pure certainty: it seems as if you now know without a single doubt which *question* to direct toward the child. But this question has no picture and cannot be put in words. This causes an initial feeling of helplessness, but it is a *mood* of nearness, of understanding, of being initiated, as it were, an "aha experience" with no conceptual content. One must be clear about one thing: the feeling of helplessness comes from having found the connection to an area of perception and relationship that is otherwise closed off to everyday consciousness. Our usual securities are meaningless there. You just have to let it happen, at first. What matters is something else: you have crossed the threshold from indirect to direct research into (the child's) being. You no longer live in the afterimages of outer perception, but rather you come into direct *contact* with the mystery entrusted to you by the child. Here understanding means not establishing facts or seeing through contexts, but rather grasping the essential in such a way that it streams directly into the will as the ability to form the world. If one regularly sets oneself into connection with this source of strength, interaction with the child (who herself *is* this source) will gradually become an interaction that dignifies, and the overall attitude of education and upbringing will become one that heals. Our body language changes, our voice, our gaze; we begin inwardly to accompany the child with different, that is, fairer thoughts and feelings. The intuitive certainty of right action at the right time grows, and alongside that the ability *also* grows to see better through circumstances in the customary sense. We rid ourselves of the habit of immediately evaluating circumstances before having properly become aware of them. A healthy antipathy sets in against presumptions and opinions. If during the poetic phase of reverent devotion to the picture we had found ourselves in the *presentiment* of crossing the threshold (approach), now that the picture has lost its charm and even its meaning, instead of which the *feeling of the decisive question—* that imageless feeling of understanding—emerges, crossing the threshold has now been *consummated* (contact). Every minute we tarry in this mood, which in the beginning is still quite seldom and ephemeral, is precious. It communicates itself to the child, although she is not physically present, as consolation and encouragement. The person who practices in this way will notice how his or her sense for artistically educational situations gradually becomes finer and his or her relationship to the child becomes brighter: it *clears up.*

In summary, we have a path for the practice of education as an art that contains four aspects, whereby the steps made while practicing need not be taken in strict sequence, but rather in living alternation. To write down one's experiences and to immerse oneself in them, one needs about twenty minutes on a few days of the week, as well as periods one inserts when one can, for the purpose of accompanying a child's play in the way described. While doing so, it is good if one can engage in some simple and calm manual activity of one's own. A mother with her sewing or knitting, and next to her the child in deep play—that has primal character, and such primal pictures need to be fetched back into reality. Of course, one needs to take the time to do so. Anyone who does not take time for his child neglects him, no question. The question is only: how does one use the time sensibly that one has managed to take for oneself? I will make a suggestion here that is most economical, when seen in a certain way. One achieves a lot without having outwardly to do anything special; but the child has the precious experience: "My parents are *interested* in me. They enjoy simply being near me." This is an unbelievable builder of trust. In particular, the so-called difficult children need our quiet, unspectacular, as it were stoic devotion, the warmth stream of modest participation. So often do they bring the unspoken plea to us: "Please just be there for me once in a while, without wanting anything, without stalking me, without criticizing me, without suspicions, expectations, judgments, worried and disappointed looks." Just being there is *healing*, provided one makes clear to oneself that in this case doing nothing outwardly is a *question of shaping*, which (for example) can be answered in the way described in this chapter. Of course there are other possibilities,[72] and in principle *any* kind of unforced togetherness with the child can become a celebration of understanding nearness, if the adult can find the inner attitude that has been characterized from different angles in this book.

Attentive but not curious, entirely devoted but not pushy presence is a *prerequisite* and a *goal*. The more frequently the following steps are made, the better this first one succeeds. It is as it were already set down to anticipate the second one, that is, the condensed description of one or more details (after-study, poetic distinction); I would like to call this step *gathering*. In the third step the image expressed in words is deepened and heightened, best through repeated and slow speaking while at the same time intensively striving to envision the scene as a picture; in this way one attains an *approach* to the actual event of understanding. This takes place if the picture dies and thus *contact* becomes possible. Ideally, one ought to carry the mood of having been touched (the question that has become certainty) into every encounter with the child as a matter of course, and one ought to learn *always*—with no particular intention—to see through inner gathering (through the eyes of a haiku poet) and imitatively to feel one's way into what one has perceived.[73] Then what has been described here as organized practice will have become an artistic habit. The different portions of the exercise would fall into one, as if a certain fundamental agreement between attention and understanding had been struck the moment the child appeared. This agreement would consist of intoning: encounter, gathering, approach, contact. One can approach this state of artistic/educational competency that has gone over into flesh and blood. Persons of the caliber of Janusz Korczak actually did attain this level. But as a rule we are subject to so many contrary influences and distractions (not just from without, but from our own inner life, as well), that I urgently recommend that one be systematic in one's practice. One will notice then whether and to what extent one can dispense with a systematic approach as one progresses.

☞15☜
No Child Is Bad

We have to bid farewell to our habitual standards of measuring value and meaning. If the child sees something more precious in a rusty nail than in an expensive piece of jewelry, then the rusty nail *is* more precious. I must by understanding live my way into the child's preferences, and initially that means accepting them. Then, I must make them my own and explore from *inside* the relationship to the world in which they are founded. Why should not the ability to forget one's entire surroundings at the sight of a quietly burning candle and to fully immerse oneself into the mystery of the flame be esteemed as highly as some fabulous intellectual, musical, or athletic performance? Anyone who has ever watched a child with a so-called behavior disorder playing beside a brook at sunset, all alone with the water, the stones and the wind, quiet, attentive, even reverently devoted to the elements, will become at least very reserved and reflective regarding the diagnosis hyperactive, or ADS (attention deficit syndrome) that may have been imposed on this child after a purely scientific test procedure. Why should the scene at the water be a *less* forceful statement than the research results obtained under laboratory conditions? We will need to switch from giving priority to the detection of the child's deficits to discovering his strengths and beauties and supporting and strengthening these by working with them. It becomes quite clear here that completely new qualities of the imagination and of flexibility will have to assert themselves in pedagogical circles, as will unconventional ways of reacting to abnormalities and of disregarding miserable normalcy. "Let a thousand flowers blossom!" The nature of schooling and upbringing requires the greatest possible freedom and variety, including legal and economic security for smaller and larger projects that are conceived of *in terms of particular children*. "Why the great words; they are not great." Adapting these words of Samuel Beckett, one could ask: Why the great educational goals? They are not great. In view of the mystery, they shrink to the point of insignificance. It is a beautiful and worthwhile task if as a parent, teacher, or therapist one no longer calls a difficult child difficult but rather acknowledges this child's *special nature* and seeks it out with "reverence for what is small" (Steiner). It would be a crass misunderstanding if one were to assume that this effort served a better assertion of educational intentions. What it serves is *understanding* as the only legitimate educational intention.

It is estimated that today about five percent of all children demonstrate an unnatural penchant for violence and recklessness as early as preschool or lower school age. The rate has risen sharply in the last fifteen years. It is well known that the same holds for violence in youth. Parallel to the increase in these tendencies toward violence, the social climate has changed to the effect that all modes of behavior and attitudes that belong to the "anatomy of human destructiveness" (Erich Fromm) are once again becoming undisputably socially acceptable, which means that they have been fully rehabilitated from the attempt of an ethical, socially artistic, and ecological change of course during the 1960s and 1970s. Whoever does not try to get at the foundation of things may call that coincidence, if they want to. A deeper examination based on developmental psychology demonstrates that children with so-called aggressive behavior disturbances are trying *to come to terms with reality*. By forming themselves into the circumstances, they take up what in the way of contemporary tint comes to meet their *inner* need to imitate (that is, the ubiquitous mood of latent animosity). Or they just let themselves *be taken hold of* by it, whereby their actual motive is the *enlightenment* (individualization) of the given darkness that they assimilate by means of imitation. Hence, their true motive is transformation. One must take into account at all times this artistic intention in the process of assimilation. Children come to terms with the animosity of the times in a participatory way: they initially *live their way into* this element by resorting to the corresponding potential of their natural endowments. In order to understand a phenomenon, one calls on what is most similar to it in one's own disposition. One may assume that in truth these children have at their disposal extraordinary powers of *courage*. They are born dragon fighters and are different from those who react to the same signs of the times with grief or fear (which points to other qualities). Aggressive children, too, are anxious and distressed, but they take it upon themselves to slip into the dragon's skin, which of course is risky business. The motive of transformation can get stuck. With regard to this, so much depends on how the adult contact persons react, think, feel, whether they see in this little Rumpelstiltskin a disturbed child or the daring little fighter who, because he has overestimated his own powers, has gotten into something that is stronger than he and that is threatening to gain dominance over him. It would be the mission of an education and upbringing that *understands* and consciously distances itself from the Zeitgeist to hold in esteem the *courageous* quality in this kind of behavior, rather than humiliating the child, who has gotten into trouble for selfless reasons, with condescending judgment. Courage must be guided to take a creative course! There must be no doubt that a child is *never* bad. He is definitely wrestling with evil, but *always* with the deep yearning to effect transformation and redemption. The incarnation impulse itself *is*, after all, this yearning, as has been extensively put forth in previous chapters. But we have also seen that this yearning cannot be fulfilled without the involvement of the initiated chosen (adult) companion.

This is where the question arises as to how often in the life of a difficult child an adult has truly, perseveringly, understandingly, and *reverently* held this child in esteem and with the inner attitude that Steiner characterizes as awe and devotion, gratitude and respect of freedom, rather than stigmatizied the child with the epithet "difficult" and constantly *looked at her* as such, whether at home, in the kindergarten, or at school; how often someone rather than crossing oneself in front of the little devil and considering suitable methods of exorcism, has stood before her in quiet admiration and acknowledgement and seen her beauty. The evil comes from outside, unsolicited but unavoidable, and takes hold of the child; the good comes not from outside, but from the child herself, and takes hold of the world, takes hold of *us*—but only if we call it out. We call it out by learning to *see* it. That is the meaning of understanding confirmation. *In truth,* "difficult" children do not exist.

☙16☙
Hope and Tragedy, or
Was Beethoven a Mistake?

If a meaningful life meant the same thing as a life of pure happiness and satisfaction, thus a life as free as possible from conflict and suffering, most of the great works of art and poetry and many groundbreaking achievements in knowledge would have to be evaluated as products of senselessness and their authors as failures. In other words, whoever wants to bring up people who are satisfied and who live in harmony with themselves and the world is striving, whether he wants this or not, for loss of the soul and abolition of the great tales (in Neil Postman's sense of the word). Shaping one's life as shallow entertainment literature? Was Georg Trakl a regrettable case? Hölderlin a mishap? Albert Camus a breakdown? Beethoven a mistake? All these artists and many others (how famous they have become does not matter) stood with overflowing warmth in the midst of the coldness of the times and tried to accomplish the *impossible*: to remain faithful to the *child*. When I say impossible, I do not mean senseless. There is a willing that points beyond the threshold. From the standpoint of this side, such willing is "impossible"; but such willing does set signs of hope here and now and is directed toward enablement further down the road. This, in the understanding of the expanded concept of childhood, is childlike willing. As the center of the human makeup,[74] it is the *child* who establishes the connection between the incarnate I (ego) and the unborn I (spirit self), thus the connection of the human being who ages forward in time and uses himself up, makes himself guilty, with his super-temporal essence of hope. Seen from a consciousness contingent on time, this super-temporal element comes to meet him from out of the future, out of the space of innocence. (The future is the space of innocence. There can be no such thing as future guilt.) In other words: where the Human Being in his primal form, the Human Being who reaches up to the spirit self, communicates himself to the individual human being and lights up within the incarnate "I," thus where *pure* hope awakens within transient existence, the *child* is at work as the relayer. This exchange can take place at any time and in any person. It actually *does* take place, constantly and more or less consciously, in every human being.[75] It finds its highest and purest expression, though, between conception and birth, in the process of incarnation, and in the initiation of the companion of the child's destiny through the child herself.

Looking for meaning also means becoming acquainted with tragedy. To speak about it in the climate of the hedonistic "okay game" is inappropriate, but necessary nonetheless. A tragic field arises when the *child* becomes aware of the other-worldliness and thus of the impossibility of his innermost willing. This is when he wants to despair, when the *fundamental contradiction* becomes evident. It consists of the fact that the child's chosen goal for life surpasses this life, that only the *wish itself* can be inserted into the context of the world on this side of the threshold, the hope rather than its actual fulfillment. That is a deeply troubling experience, which, at the same time, reveals a liberating aspect of the mystery: warmth and movement at having been designed according to the Human Being (the power of hope) are the qualities that point beyond the finite—the point of death—precisely because of their point of reference in the impossible. This explains the seemingly nonsensical but nevertheless evident connection between experiencing senselessness and awakening to hope (archetypal in the crisis of puberty[76]). I mean hope *proper*, that does not attach itself to this or that goal, but which has the character of an altered faculty of perception. One sees the world as it were in a super-worldly light or through the eyes of the *child*. Under earthly circumstances, the tragic field *is* the field of hope. This observation is not meant to make depression and feelings of deadly boredom with life seem harmless. But the escalation of the crisis of hope—or, as the case may be, the crisis of sense—to the point of suicide could certainly be hindered in many cases by means of the experience of protecting, accompanying, consoling and encouraging help from other people, of *being recognized* and *acknowledged*. This experience, either during childhood or later, can set the tone for encounters with the dimension of the tragic. To want to *avert* such an encounter might possibly lead straight to failure when things get serious. So many people who not only grew beyond themselves in the tragic fundamental conflict, but in the end were tragically broken, were further burdened with the role of being the difficult, peculiar child, whose bad end one saw coming and tried with all means at one's disposal to prevent! Even if in such cases the educators did not pull out *all* the stops of forced pedagogical happiness, being branded as a failure, a disappointment who plunges his parents into feelings of guilt can in retrospect prove to have been a great calamity in the course of an unusual life. In a threshold situation, it just might tip the balance between hope and longing for death in the wrong direction. And yet, this is exactly why those who end their own lives in despair deserve our unreserved respect. "Every child has the right to its own death," according to one of the most *mysterious* statements by Janusz Korczak. Even a death that goes beyond our ability to comprehend it and leaves us filled with grief and helplessness must not be considered just a misfortune. It can be part of the mystery. Let the departed one confer over the sense or nonsense of the life he has lived and the way it ended with those higher beings with whom he once conferred over his coming. What do *we* know?[77]

Conclusion

Rule of Thumb for Proportionality:

Always permit a child *twice* as many bad manners, ineptitudes, fears, and mood swings as you allow yourself. Consider: children *cannot hide half as much* as you.

The Will to Form Oneself:

The child's will to form herself cannot be *disposed*. It is *singular* (always unique) and *directed* toward the Human Being, which is sculpturally pre-designed in the child. This entelechy of hope, which is indistinguishably common to everyone, does *not* contradict the individual character of the biographical directional impulse. Rather, it confirms it, because the individual is the highest possible earthly shine of the all-connecting Human Being. The individuality is free towards an all-human goal, with and by which it is inspired. This goal, *essentially* described, is the Christ. The individual contributes in an inimitable and induplicable way to the enablement of the Human Being (the nearness of Christ), because no two people tread the same path under the same preconditions. The path is the question. Each child incorporates a never-asked question of the human being to the Human Being. Education under contempt for or neglect of the idea of childhood thus outlined cuts the organism of society off from the *socio-sculptural stream of ideas*, since this stream originates qualitatively in the same source as the faculty to educate artistically. The *essence of childhood* connects all bodily children and lives in all people as the awakened or unawakened sense for the future, which is directed toward thou (and, as described, is developed through the value discerning view). When this faculty is not in effect where pedagogical encounters take place, a wasteland arises a zone, as it were, where interactions between the outer social life and the inner origin of impulses of social form dry up.

The Principle of Practicality:

About the principle of practicality and the pragmatic desolation that sets in with the desolation of the life of education, Joseph Beuys tersely said, "Sculpture is quite simply a concept of the future, and woe unto those conceptions that have not assimilated this concept."

Karma Can Be Viewed Together with Freedom

... only if one understands them both as *future* effectiveness, i.e., if one sees karmic quality in the *ideals* that a person follows, in the *abilities* to which he trains himself for the sake of doing justice to these ideals, and in the *obstacles* that he overcomes for the sake of attaining these abilities. That is a fully different thought than if one describes karma in a monocausal-linear mode of thought as an unavoidable force that dictates from out of the past and/or pushes in from the outside. No one should talk about destiny who has not understood that the birth of a child (the process of incarnation) is the importation of the *future*.

The Child Is not Formed by Circumstance

Rather, he forms himself into his circumstances. Anyone who wants to put off this distinction as sophism does not recognize how far-reaching it is. From the perspective of archetypal phenomena, environmental influences are not *formative* forces, but rather *de*forming ones. This is because, to the extent that the child's soul is woven together with the world, it is subject to dividuation (dismemberment). Seen from this side, it is not a limited configuration, but rather one that disperses itself in every direction and is in a state of dissolution. By contrast, the child's soul *individualizes itself* to the extent that it escapes circumstances and enters a plane of gathering apart from them. Dismemberment (environment, sense world) and gathering (inner world, supersensible world) are the poles between which the soul oscillates. Self-formation takes place out of *gathering*. The gathering point lies in the future—this means, paradoxically, in the prenatal sphere. The zone of dispersion is the zone of the past in space and time, the *finished world*. Nothing is *formed* out of it. The fact that we must go all the way back to a person's beginnings in the course of his life, in order to find the gathering point in the future, is one of the world's great mysteries.

When a Child Enters the World,

. . . the soul emerges from a state of existence in which *hope* amounts to the air the soul breathes. It is an air that has the character of *light*. This light is a formative light: *it brings things to manifestation*. What it brings to light can be called *aspects of hope:* qualities of being that occur as pure experiences: the experience of what is solid, dependable (certainty); the experience of what is flowing and streaming, clingy and adaptable (partiality, shelter, the ability to transform); the experience of what is light, freely mobile, what takes hold of and fills space (abandon, joy); the experience of what warms, of what glows and brightens, enflames (power, brightness, development). These four aspects of hope, which can only combine where everything is bathed in the radiance of love, configure the human being in the incarnation process as a physical-bodily being, a formative-flowing being, a being of breath and mobility, of warmth and will. And they outwardly encounter anew the child who is living her way into earthly circumstances as a natural (divine) creation: earth, water, air, light/warmth/fire. This encounter with the elements is the actual "religion" of the child: she experiences herself through them in her being reconnected ("religio") with the sphere of hope from which she comes. Every sense experience in interaction with the elements, with nature, is a memory of the spiritual world, an event of hope. The fact that today so many children are fearful and troubled, roaming around in restless search of something, constantly feeling dissatisfied and needy, as if they were suffering some chronic lack, has to do with the fact that the divine creation is being pushed back by human creation. The elemental fields of experience are becoming rare. This removes a large part of the nourishment of hope for the soul. To equalize this undernourishment of the soul is one of the central tasks of an education of the future that is oriented *toward the child*.

Notes

1n. I took care of Jessica in a children's home. She would fall into a terrible panic whenever jet planes would fly through the sky above us. For her, they were beings. When I wrote this poem for Jessica, she was twelve years old.

2n. A very angry little six-year-old who is easily beside himself shouts at his father as the two argue violently: "You always yell at me when I'm having a temper tantrum!"

3n. When the fearful eleven-year-old girl who never wants to be alone and still only lets her parents go out in the evening with the greatest reluctance, hears once how underage her behavior is ("You're behaving like a baby!"), she retorts: "Like a baby? But I have to take care of you!"

4n. Authors' names in parentheses refer to the list of works cited in the bibliography.

5n. Libertarian = aimed at self determination.

6n. *The evaluative view* causes fear.

7n. *Intentional education* is deceptive education.

8n. The term "century of the child" goes back to a book of the same name published by Ellen Keys in 1902, which at that time made an impact similar to the way Neill's theory and practice of antiauthoritarian education would sixty years later.

9n. The battle cry of "political correctness" is aimed at a socially engaged body of parents and teachers who unflaggingly maintain certain human ideals.

10n. When I wrote this poem, Mariella was ten years old and was considered "resistant to education."

11n. "Integral" in the sense of Jean Gebser, "intuitive" in Rudolf Steiner's sense.

12n. As opposed to stepping into the indeterminateness of actually devoting oneself to something.

13n. He may do so by seeing "defects" where I am confronted by substantial and/or momentous existential questions, which cannot occur without a feeling of helplessness.

14n. Sophie had good reason to be sad frequently and inwardly secluded. She found refuge in my family for a while. When I wrote this poem she was eight years old.

15n. Johannes Stüttgen

16n. Rudolf Steiner

17n. The two ineptitudes, examined more closely, turn out to be one and the same.

18n. The capacity has to do with thinking and light; the wish with feeling and warmth; the drive with willing and fire.

Footnotes

1.   The fast-and-easy esoteric scene has renamed starkly self-centered means of motivation as "positive thinking." It has a tranquilizer concept of health (it conflates health with a pleasurable, worry-free meander of life) and a choice of therapies that is as countless as it is ominous. This groove is for the most part a movement of bandwagon riders and yes-men with no sense of social discrimination. The "New Age" and the "New World Order" have aligned. Those portions of the scene that could be classified as belonging to the left-alternative movement, and that sought to combine social change with spirituality, have become nearly invisible. "Esotericism goes Disneyland" (Rainer Kakuska in *Psychology Today*). One can encounter fascist tendencies in the esoteric scene, but they do not have nearly as much weight as some dogmatic zealots on the left would have us believe. To attempt to connect Anthroposophy with Fascism is a campaign of slander and misinformation that leaves one speechless. I say this as one of the few anthroposophists who has always been open to the antiauthoritarian (non-Marxist) left and who thereby was and still is hypersensitive toward one-sidedly rightist or even fascist activities wherever they occur.

2.   We need to acquaint even children and youth with the pathological tendencies of our times to such extent and in such a way that they are able to come to terms with them *on*

the basis of their own sound judgment. We do not promote such a capacity for judgment by merely restricting, prohibiting, or demonizing. Children not only feel led astray when we tell them that television "leaves you damaged." They actually know living counter-examples, such as fellow students or friends who, despite occasional consumption of television, are obviously fully healthy, and do not demonstrate any other conspicuous abnormalities. We waste our credibility through generalizations of this kind. Irrespective of television, entertainment music, computers, comics, or teenage publications, a child that grows up in an atmosphere of social warmth, is shown respect, who receives sufficient nourishment in the form of stories, fairy tales, music, and so forth, and whose creative faculties are supported, will come away unscathed from regulated encounters with anything. All we need to do is derive the proper age criteria from the pedagogical study of man, add our input to the selection process (even in the field of media/fast food/entertainment there are considerable differences in quality), set time limits, provide enough counter-offers, and above all stand at our children's and teenagers' sides with interest, willingness to communicate, and expert advice. Expert advice and generalized condemnation are mutually exclusive. What is dangerous is when children plunge into illusionary pseudo-worlds and technological deception too early, without moderation, and unsupervised. Once more: not everything the entertainment world offers is inferior or harmful. There are remarkably creative achievements in film, radio drama, and in rock music, to name only a few examples. Many computer games are quite intelligent. And occasional pleasurable excursions into the world of Donald Duck or the land of the invincible Gauls have never ruined any child, even if their character-building value is virtually null. It is our task to help children and teenagers encounter these options in a controlled rather than an addictive way (they are, in tendency, addictive), and to learn to separate the wheat from the chaff. To this end, they must deal with the chaff *as well*—bearing in mind of course that there are limitations to what is constructive in the end. Our stance in the face of activities offered or engaged in out of contempt for humanity must be uncompromising. As far as the use of the media is concerned, normally we can approximate general age criteria within reason. But in addition, we must always take into account the particular nature and situation of the child in question. Parents who are uncertain themselves should seek advice.

3.   It is regrettable and even tragic that no or only very limited dialog ever came about between the antiauthoritarian movement, with its autonomous "children's shops," and the advocates of social threefolding and Waldorf education. In Anthroposophy, the enthusiastic friends of childhood who were inspired by A. S. Neill could have found the carrying fundamental spirituality they lacked, for Rudolf Steiner was *the* thinker of the twentieth century to buttress the concepts of "freedom" and "dignity" using an actual study of the human being, and in so doing to lift them out of the realm of merely relative ethical postulates. In turn, the fresh and unconventional wind that was wafting through the antiauthoritarian scene, its joy in experimentation, its suspicion of antiquated forms, would have done the anthroposophists good. But the fear of coming into contact was too great. Here is not the place to go into the reasons in depth. Two streams with much in common in the way of fundamental intent missed each other all along the line, which in my opinion contributed to the demise of the one, which was young, dynamic, and unconsumed, while the other, looking back on long experience, never found the way out of its tendency toward convention nor back to its own source, which was steeped in freedom and social reform. Soon, an emotional and perhaps

embittered battle will rage once more over the question of education in connection with the botched development of society. There are signs of this already, and it is to be hoped that this time the Waldorf movement will without reservation be on the side of other efforts which, like itself, are in favor independence, and whose interest is to take its cue not from political plans or demands to supply the economy with human "material," but exclusively from the needs and the being of the child.

4.   It is not a seldom occurrence that faculties in Waldorf schools or Waldorf kindergartens place in doubt the results of evaluations made by anthroposophically oriented *practices for curative education and educational counseling* by means of reasoning such as: "In this case, we need a scientifically founded diagnosis made by *genuine specialists*." This happens whenever the assessment based on anthroposophical study of man does not supply the "problem" diagnosis that the teachers want. Laments of this sort can be heard at the annual specialists' conference for outpatient curative education. (This conference has taken place since 1993 alternately at the Janusz Korczak Institut Wolfschlugen and at the Bernard Lievegoed Work Community in Wahlwies, with an average of 120 participants from all parts of Germany.) According to many newly founded practices for curative education and educational counseling, and contrary to all expectations, collaboration with Waldorf institutions has proven *more difficult* than with public schools, youth welfare departments, and so forth. What is happening here? There is clearly a deficit in mutual perception and understanding which urgently needs to be dealt with.

5.   The notion of the defective human being will only be overcome once and for all if and when the higher senses are developed, in particular the I-sense (suggested reading for a basic understanding: Rudolf Steiner, *The Twelve Senses*, Steiner

Press, New York). The fully developed activity of the I-sense is the ability to comprehend others in their uncorrupted and incorruptible "higher I" in such a way that the entire body of the perceiver, which trembles delicately even in the activity of breathing and metabolizing, becomes a sounding board for the "resonating" of the Other. When this occurs, the Other is no longer *foreign*, despite any difference. Initial ways to practice this still distant capacity of perception, which will ultimately lead to the unfolding of direct *healing forces*, are described in Part 2, as "Suggestions for Upbringing and Education as an Art Form."

6.　　Cf. "In Conclusion": "The child is not formed out of the circumstances surrounding him/her. . . ."

7.　　Paul Feyerabend writes about this in his book *Erkenntnis für freie Menschen* (*Knowledge for Free Human Beings*) (Frankfurt 1980): "The Mystic who is able to leave his body through his own power is doubtless hardly impressed when two carefully trained, but not particularly intelligent people manage, through the support of thousands of scientific slaves and billions of dollars, to take a few clumsy steps on a dry rock (the Moon). [He will much rather] lament the decline of the spiritual capacities of humanity. One can of course laugh oneself to death over this objection, but there are no *arguments* against it. The objection that the so-called mystics . . . are deluded is a rhetorical cliché, because it cannot be justified. On the other hand, a number of gnostics have declared matter to be an illusion, so that from their perspective the travelers to the Moon are the deluded ones. Once more, as much as one can laugh about this viewpoint, one can make no argument against it."

8.　　For Hillmann/Ventura (see list of works cited), "acorn" stands for what is undeveloped but yet to come, and which itself creates the conditions it needs to develop (loosely according to Stüttgen; see Chapter 5, quote from *Siebentausend Eichen* (*Seven Thousand Oaks*).

9.   In my book I have designated Hillmann's and Ventura's conception of the "secondary and contingent" as "primary and secondary determination" (Chapter 5), in contrast to the "directional impulse of an individual's biography" (whose guardian is the angel).

10.   Without wanting to anticipate the reader's own imagination, I would like to draw her attention the fact that Kai is obviously a child who is 1) linguistically gifted, 2) attentively observant, 3) imaginative and inventive, 4) empathetic and considerate, 5) self-critical (and has been from early on). Furthermore, he is afraid of sober reality, objectivity (i.e., what cannot be changed) and being alone, that is, he strongly seeks social, community connection, although he on the other hand can be by himself with no problem, as long as there is someone nearby. To find a clue, one can now try to speculate on a task in life that would demand a gift for language arts, attentiveness, fantasy, empathy, self-criticism, and a modicum of skepticism toward the inalterable (thus a penchant to what is in the process of undergoing development), and sociability. If one then comes up with a corresponding field of duty, one should nevertheless not commit the error of taking this literally in the profane sense, as if one had now realized what Kai's life profession is. Rather, one ought to form a *picture* of the configuration of the child's capacities or capabilities to which one can now turn, rather than simply staring at the "anxiety symptoms." One ought to appreciate and carefully promote, but remain completely open to *what* ultimately wants to come to the fore, and *how*. (I know a *technician* who by disposition is a *judge*—in the sense of "one who is just"—and who for many years has been consulted to mediate conflict situations in groups of colleagues, friends, and even in institutions to which he is a complete stranger. Everyone senses that this man is certain and uncompromising in questions of justice in everyday life, irrespective of legal para-

graphs. This is his great strength. All the same, he never became a judge, but rather a technologist. He had little aptitude for the former in the beginning, but through hard work he became an expert in this field as well, to which various apparently unfortunate circumstances had brought him. The "judge," on the other hand, has been with him since his childhood, and he can bring this talent freely to bear in every life situation, when asked.) In some cases, a grasp of the configuration of a child's talent might be a direct preview of his later choice of vocation, but that is not what matters. It must be left open; that is important. Otherwise, expectations sneak in that in turn destroy the appreciative relationship one has gained to the childhood agglomeration of capabilities. What is alone decisive is the aspect of *practicing* such image forming.

11.   The difference between a wild hypothesis and a creative one is the same as the difference, say, between a sloppily imagined fairy tale and a cohesive, "genuine" one, which talks in the form of images about *structures of the life of the human soul.*

12.   I have spoken more in depth about this in reference to Rudolf Steiner, in my book *The Human Being in Conflict between Self-Realization and Conformity*, Esslingen 1995 [not yet available in English].

13.   The poet C.W. Aigner writes about this in *Das Verneinen der Peldeluhr* [*The Negation of the Pendulum Clock*], Stuttgart, 1996:

Light Seed

Seed of stars
that tomorrow sprout
in one single
glistening blossom.

14.   What is actually being "analyzed" is whether Heinrich Himmler's creed, "Woe unto them who forget that not everyone who looks like a human being actually is one," is perhaps true in some way, after all. Currently, the most popular proponent of such "analysis" is the Australian philosopher Peter Singer (*Practical Ethics* and other books). Reading suggestions on this topic: Jens Heisterkamp, *The Biotechnical Human Being*.

15.   If "suitability for human rights" (dignity) is connected with qualities such as self awareness, autonomy, self-responsibility, reason, the individual capacity to set goals and express oneself, social competency, personality profiles, and so forth, (parameters of the value of life), no infant would have human rights. It is on just this issue that the bio-ethics inaugurated by Singer becomes not only absurd, but *malicious*, as well (I call the debasement of childhood malicious). When one leaves aside all its sophistry, it represents the point of view that a newborn human being is (as yet) no human being at all, in other words, the birth of a human being is not the birth of a human being. We beget non-humans. That is absurd, because no non-humans can be born of humans. The concept of a *"not-yet* human being" is a mere rhetorical prosthetic. If the human being came to the world as a non-human, then all human beings would at all times have come into the world as non-humans. Where, when, and how is the *human being* to have come about? Within the heads of non-humans? To put it precisely, Singer & Co. do away with the concept of the human being, and I am not sure whether it is on account of mere sloppiness of thought or not. The present book begins here and takes a radically opposite position. On this question, there are no compromises possible. We ought, in order to make the criteria clear, to quit using slogans such as, "Children must be raised to become full human beings." Every man or woman child *is* a full human being.

16.   There are those who feel obliged to defend selfishness and egotism as "healthy" attributes of the modern human being against "good person" blabber about selflessness. Such people take sides with the undisputed spirit of the times, which is in favor of the destruction of relationships. This anti-Zeitgeist has in recent decades never been seriously put on the defensive, but at least it was energetically placed in question for a while. Then the "mainstream" legend was launched by intellectuals who were tired of opposition. According to this legend, public opinion was dominated for decades by rigorous moral apostles of the alternative left. It is insolent contortion of history for the purpose of justifying the course of opportunism taken by its fabricators. They are basically ashamed of it today. Whoever is willing to stick to the facts knows that between about 1965 and 1985 there arose an outcry against the social circumstances of interpersonal relations increasingly determined by selfishness and egotism. The outcry was at the same time a cry of longing for values that went beyond selfishness and egotism. It came from portions of the youth and resounded positively among portions of the adults, but was misunderstood and denounced by others, and exploited, taken advantage of, and led astray by yet others. The outcry was never a "dominant public opinion," and now it is mute, for the time being. But that will change. Perhaps the *idea of childhood* will lead to an initial ignition (provided it is further taken up).

17.   I say "a kind of" because even the concept of autonomy can in connection with a simplistic conception of reincarnation be misunderstood in a highly materialistic way. One might then imagine that the child comes to earth with particular *images* of his coming life, which he wants unconditionally to *assert*. The autonomy of the child is an autonomy of *question*, though. Every child is unmistakable and unique in *the never-before-asked question that it puts to the HUMAN BEING.*

This question provides the biographical impulse for the direction it will take, and the basis for its autonomous implementation. For this reason, we as educators must become questioners in our own right, or, as the case may be, we must ponder on the fact that we *are* questioners. Mutual understanding between caregiver and child is possible on the level of posing questions. The process of incarnation will be further examined so that naïve fallacies along the lines of "implementation of a preconceived plan for life" no longer come into play

18.   A sort of horror comes over me at times when I am studying specialized psychological or psychiatric literature on so-called childhood behavioral disturbances, not because they say malicious things about children, but on account of a machine language they think they have to use for the sake of demonstrating scientific rigor. This terminology is condescending *as such*, evocative of a technical service for the purpose of surveilling humans. It communicates diagnoses made of the function, equipment, performance, and susceptibility of highly complicated *instruments*. I place myself in the shoes of an anxious or failing child who is brought into a strange building where he is examined, interrogated and otherwise placed under investigative scrutiny, and whereupon in this kind of language a damage control report is made to the parents. When I do this, I imagine that the child understands what is being said; hence my horror. Now the rebuttal: The children naturally do *not* understand what is being said; the fact that this language is inhuman is your *adult opinion*, and has nothing whatever to do with the children. Really? I would not be too sure of that. Children understand very well. Even if we stand behind closed doors and use words that they do not know. They understand on another level. Machine language is the expression of a certain attitude. Out of this attitude one can be neither healed nor educated; one can only be *manipulated*.

19.   We know this phenomenon in so-called difficult children quite exactly. One can experience (and learn from) what a difference it makes whether one confronts a child with the 'inspector view' and wants to make diagnostic deductions from its behavior during play, while painting, and so on, or whether one just welcomes it without wanting anything in particular, but with the inner attitude: here is the island where you are allowed to be the way you are. The inspector view has a disconcerting and shaming effect. One cannot conceal from a child an intent to pass judgment. Whenever he senses he is being judged, he immediately disguises or contorts himself, and the mask he puts on can be "good" and super-conscientious. If we meet him with an unconditional mood of welcome, with no ulterior motives—this is a skill that can be learned through patient practice—the child is immediately motivated to show *himself*. Without any mask. It is, after all, a quite pleasant and encouraging experience for a child to be regarded quietly, attentively, expectantly and with no checking up in the back of one's mind. The child feels the wish to present something "nice" to this vision. He composes himself; now the inner treasure chamber is carefully opened. . . . Many children who come to us have never been in this situation. It is something entirely new to them just to feel welcome.

20.   Cf. Chapter 3.

21.   What is meant here is not the clinical profile of autism, but rather the 'usual' problem of feeling alone in the midst of people; the relationship to the world determined by loneliness; the crisis of not being able really to have a relationship with anything or anyone. This lack of relationship is founded on a *fear* of the world that has to do with the *state* of the world.

22.   One would swiftly send a business consultant on his way who wanted to take over the whole business and sniff around

in the private affairs of the management personnel. But one sometimes tolerates official or unofficial educational counselors who usurp the authority of the entire family and interfere in their most intimate affairs. One should watch out for "experts" with an inclination to being indiscreet and giving orders. One should reject "friendly" advice that seems intimidating, humiliating, or arrogant. Anyone who takes advantage of the weaker position of one seeking advice and help for the sake of himself feeling strong and important is no more and no less than an immature person.

23.   It is self-understood that this does *not* pertain to parents who treat their children lovelessly, who neglect them, deceive them, abuse them. Such parents have squandered their privilege of destiny—which does not mean that they can never regain it. Not only do they need help, but they must also be prepared to comply with directives. Otherwise, there is no alternative than to protect their children from them.

24.   The notion of parents being chosen (by the child) seems to contradict what I said above. Chosen parents torment their child? Has the child chosen to be tormented, then? No. But the child *has* accepted as part of its choice the *prospect* of being tormented, much in the same way as a woman does who loves a man and marries him, all the while knowing he has a brutal side. Since she also knows his loving sides, though, she takes his brutal side into account, filled with the hope that she can heal him through her love. There is a power of hope active in the child, which comes from the pre-birth perception of the *pure being* of the mother and the father, and this perception weighs more than the premonition of possible disappointment. It is all the more tragic when parents do not comprehend the enormous acknowledgment that they are receiving, and reject the child's show of trust through disrespect or brutality. Just how far-reaching the implications of the tragedy of child abuse are can only be really brought home in the context of the thought that children select their parents.

25.   The concept of education as an art was not introduced by Rudolf Steiner as some nice slogan, but as a well-considered formulation meant to point toward a fully new understanding of the field of pedagogical practice. I deal with that more in depth in Chapter 5.

26.   We often experience it as an educational failure if a child cannot be spared certain painful experiences if the child goes through states of sadness or anxiety against which the parents are powerless. Suffering of this kind can be beneficial, though. Suppose the mother can only help herself by indulging her child's fear. She changes her own habits accordingly, and gives in to the child's excessive demands of proximity, devotion, shelter, pampering, and consolation. This might irritate the father, who has read about overprotective mothers and would prefer simply to train the child not to be afraid. So he withdraws, brooding. Thus there is a crisis in a marriage that until now has been virtually free of conflict. With this crisis, a process has started that leads to three positive things. First, the mother, by giving in to the child's fear, becomes aware that she herself had suffered as a child, and still does suffer, under considerable anxiety. In part, these fears have been calmed by a well-ordered middle class life style; in part she has transformed them into a sense of domestic duty; in part she applies them to the material concerns of everyday life. So by acknowledging her child's fears, she can now give in to her own. She becomes more honest toward herself and resolves to work on herself, but at the same time she begins to assert needs that she has repressed for years. Second, the marital crisis turns out to be a long-overdue chance for the parents to deal with each other in a crucial way. Their relationship had been peaceful, but it was frozen into everyday routines and formalities. Now the parents fight every once and a while, but they are handling the crisis in a productive manner, thus developing new interest

for one another and learning that marriage is a chance to form oneself and each other. Third, the child makes great strides in coming to terms with her fear. To be sure, these steps have been triggered by the mother's having begun her own process of self-contemplation and self-education, and by the resulting marital crisis. But because of her parents' positive approach to it, the child takes her steps entirely of her own accord. (By the way, this does not automatically imply that fears are always transmitted from mother to child via some kind of mechanism. A fashionable pattern of explanation, to be sure, but it is much too simplistic. Let us just assume that the child had found—and sought?—in the mother a person who knew out of her own experience what fear of life is, and was therefore able instinctively to attune herself to it. If we link this assumption with the notion of parents being chosen by their children, quite different connections emerge.) The parents' supposed failure has led in this case to their refraining from wanting to eliminate the child's (symptoms of) fear and to taking themselves to task instead. This has proven healing for all parties involved. First, the child felt understood and accepted in her fear; second, her parents freed her by refraining from acting on their own pedagogical ambitions, and third, she experienced the new beginning in her mother's life and in her parents' relationship as an *encouragement*.

27.   The sculptural event is the "push toward something futuristic, which wants out of itself to become form in matter" (Johannes Stüttgen in *Thinkers, Artists, Revolutionaries*, Wangen 1995).

28.   Werner Kuhfuss writes in the April 1994 issue of the periodical *Wege* (ed. Anton Kimpfler) that "what makes children disobedient at ever younger ages today is not lack of strictness on the part of adults. Rather, is it the lack of sound images of the world, a lack that sclerotically permeates us

all, teachers included. The children sense this deterioration. And they cause commotion out of despair." The *first* thing we need in this connection is a "sound image" of the world *of childhood itself.*

29.　　I have never found Bettelheim's writings on education entirely convincing. But he did contribute a lot to acknowledging the nurturing quality of fairy tales, and to the cause for so-called difficult children. That in itself does him honor. The things about him that began to surface after his suicide are of no interest to me. I find pitiful how fashionable it has become to throw after a deceased great mind all the weakness, everyday erring, and hypocrisy that can be found about them, for the purpose of diminishing their work, let alone the truth or falsehood of what is being thrown. Let him who is without sin throw the first stone.

30.　　The fact that a more complex concept of beauty is in play here than the conventional notion is something I have dealt with in my book *Jugend im Zwiespalt* in the Chapter "Vom Urvertrauen in die Schönheit," [not currently available in English]. Beauty in a deeper sense is *what is just.* To do justice to an issue or an entity means to allow it to manifest in its beauty. Even a rusty nail is beautiful if the work of art needs it in order to make itself understood. *Because* the work of art needs it, it is beautiful.

31.　　The fact that some people make it through the most adverse childhood circumstances to become creative, idealistically tempered personalities is probably the most striking proof of how real is the individual impulse of biographical direction. But no one would derive the idea that one has to wish sickness upon people one loves, or cause them misery or grief, from the fact that a person can grow through illness and grief. The same holds for overtly or covertly restrictive or intentional education. It can mobilize an individual's will to take form – if he's lucky. But that does not entitle us to try it out on children in the spirit of an experiment, or to use it to justify our own lack of effort to understand. The best and surest way to encourage a child for his path in life is the attitude characterized in this book as "understanding confirmation."

32.   By that I mean first of all that committees need to be established that originate in the educational sphere and are not beholden to party politics. These committees should be manned by persons experienced in educating and child rearing, parents included, of course. These committees would have the authority to intervene in all important political decisions regarding which they gain the impression that these decisions would put children and youth at a disadvantage. Second, I mean that advocates of childhood and youth *with no political or economic interests* need to be commissioned at municipal, regional, state/provincial and federal levels. These advocates should come from the ranks of the proposed committees and need to have at their disposal a dedicated budget for *child-worthy* projects. The advocates would decide on concrete purposes for which this money was to be spent in collaboration with *councils for childhood and youth* formed for that express purpose. Thirdly, I mean that all politicians responsible for questions of education and child rearing would have to have completed some kind of formal training in education, or at least a practical internship at a suitable facility, and would be obligated to engage in continuing education on a regular basis in the fields of education, developmental psychology, special education, or fundamentals of children's health and healing. First steps in this direction could be taken today. It would be worth the effort. In the long run, though, the success of this model would depend on entirely new modes of educational thought being developed in an *independent life of education*. These suggestions for reconfiguring education are sketchy and provisional, to be sure; but they do indicate the necessary direction.

33.   Rudolf Steiner designates the astral stream issuing from the future of the body and flowing counter to the course of time as the current of love and hate, desires, interest, wishing, and so forth, (*Psychosophy* lectures, 1910). In normal life, it is the flow of desire and wishing between love and hate; in life from conception to birth, it is the stream of *pure love*. It only becomes polarized *under earthly circumstances*. But being maintained in the stream of pure love is a state that never becomes lost *entirely*. One can always turn back toward it.

34.   An especially demanding and knowledgeable book on this subject is Dieter E. Zimmer, *Tiefenschwindel* (*Negative Vertigo*), Reinbek, 1990 [not currently available in English]. To be sure, Zimmer would presumably take Anthroposophy apart the same as he did psychoanalysis. His standpoint is, after all, rational criticism of science, and one must penetrate deeply into Anthroposophy to recognize that it rests on thorough (to the point of being boundary shattering) work in thought. Nevertheless, anyone in pursuit of an anthroposophical psychology or psychotherapy that is *linked to psychoanalysis*, and that expands and supplements it (such attempts to square the circle do exist), ought to read Zimmer's book.

35.   Cf. Chapter 14 *Seeds of Ability*.

36.   There is a big difference between looking for possibilities to prevent hereditary predispositions and wanting to preemptively eradicate "deviant behavior" because it is not in keeping with conventional standards. Anyone on the quest for the latter needs to make clear to himself that he would be working toward a complete standstill of the evolution of the human mind. After all, anything that was ever new has always announced itself through deviating behavior, in other words through *transitional phases of human consciousness*. Everybody knows that countless people who were ahead of their time have awakened the suspicion in the surrounding

world that they were "not in their right minds." No matter how great the intolerance may have been and regardless of how it was articulated, cultural progress has always taken place in the conflict between mediocre thinking, feeling, willing and extraordinary, marginalized, alienated contemporaries, at the sight of whom the question arose whether to categorize them as sick or insane, or as avant-gardes, pioneers or visionaries. Are times now approaching when this age-old topic will be done away with by forcing unusual people to be normal in the fetal state?

37.   One such means of manipulation that has become absolutely normal is the administration of Ritalin. Ritalin is an stimulant given for states of restlessness and nervousness. A portion of so-called hyperactive children react to this medication, paradoxicaly by becoming more sedate. Their systems are deceived, in a way. The drug takes advantage of an effect that is comparable to what happens when fidgety children placed in front of a TV, of all things, and confronted by pure frenzy, come to rest (and flip out all the more afterward). Since the dosage of Ritalin can be maintained at such a low level that no bodily addiction is established, objections to this "therapy" are becoming fewer and fewer. Intervention into the biochemistry of the brain and the composition of the blood alters the constitution of the soul and the long-term behavior of the child. Thus adults do with children exactly what substance abusers do with themselves. The latter want to alter their own feel for their lives and bodies through ingestion of a substance because they do not come to terms with themselves in their unaltered state. The former, by administering a substance, alter the child's feel for life and his body, because they do not come to terms with *him* in its unaltered state. The little fidgeters would have no problems with *themselves*, overall, if only their environment could manage with them. It is a seamy assertion to claim that they suf-

fer *under their own condition*. What really happens—irrespective of the issue of addiction—is that drugs are administered with the objective of making the children subservient. We should at least openly admit this, rather than constantly drivel about "healing" and "responsibility for the well-being of the child." Only those who are not deceived by the actual ethical and therapeutic significance of their actions have a standard of measurement for circumstances under which something that is irresponsible in principle must be done anyway, in a specific situation. Such a person will if at all possible avoid medication, and if there is no getting around it, she will medicate only with a sense of defeat that it cannot be avoided. What normally happens, though, is that treatment with Ritalin is considered in many places to be downright obligatory. Parents are put under pressure; the way it works is so convincing. This reveals all the misery of the current conception of therapy. The claim is that Ritalin improves the prerequisites for psychotherapy. Permit me to say that is utter nonsense, because the therapeutic situation caused by medicinal alteration is an *illusion*.

38.   Pertaining to the temperaments (distinguishing the four basic types phlegmatic, melancholic, sanguine, and choleric), their manifestation has indeed become less definite than only a few years ago. It has been helpful in curative educational diagnostics to ask what temperament the child definitely does *not* have, rather than which predominates. As a rule, so-called difficult children display an overlapping of three temperamental colorations in a specific conglomeration while the fourth is not at all discernible, or only slightly. If, say, a child that displays phlegmatic, choleric, and melancholic features, but entirely lacks the sanguine element, this is a place where we can carefully apply a process of learning and supplementation.

39.　　On death in the context of Josef Beuys, c.f. Johannes Stüttgen, *Zeitstau* (*Build-up of Time*), Stuttgart 1988, lectures 1 and 2, [not currently available in English]. On the banishment of death: H. E. Richter, *Umgang mit Angst* (*Dealing with Death*), Hamburg 1992, [not currently available in English]. Rudolf Steiner: "Über das Ereignis des Todes und Tatsachen der nachtodlichen Zeit" ("About the Event of Death and Facts of Time after Death"), 1916.

40.　　I mean "material" in a broad sense: weaponry, nuclear power plants and waste, drugs and medicines, film material, material with which to conduct debates. The principles of explosion (tearing to bits), disfigurement (deformation), withdrawal (illusion) dominate and desolate the field of relationships, impart direction to thinking, feeling and willing, and take form in the inventories mentioned above. We accumulate explosive capacities (in response to a dark urge) to deal with growing sclerotic tendencies, to enable the ultimate blow of liberation (blowing the earth to bits). Against mechanization, we summon the *dream of* conjured (blissful chaos, storm and oblivion, disintegration, lack of control, blackness); against the cultural terror of utilitization we deploy the withdrawal into illusion, starting with Hollywood and ending with schemes to make the world happy and dreams of belonging among the select few. In order to preempt misunderstanding regarding the idea of disfigurement, I do not mean anything that tends towards "decadence"; rather, I agree with Franz Dahlem, who once said, "What is beautiful? What we do not allow to deteriorate." In other words, a thing, a matter, a person becomes beautiful through our taking care of him or her. It all depends on esteem. No other concept of beauty exists at the end of the twentieth century.

41.　　I permit myself to abbreviate as a force field of cold or the trinity of "counterforces" or "adversaries" described by Rudolf Steiner and which he designated as luciferic, ahrimanic, and asuric.

42.   Cf. *Seven Thousand Oaks*, Josef Beuys, ed. Groener/ Kaendler, Cologne 1987, as well as *Conversations about Trees*, ed. Rainer Rappmann, Wangen 1993. One can interpret a "tree planting initiative," along with Beuys, as any deed done in the spirit of "The Moving One" (Christ) by human beings for the sake of the Human Being, the freedom configuration of the social organism. Thus, any creative deed. Of course, the term also means quite concretely that the social sculpture will be a world forestation action, too ("forestation, not administration"). On the concept of creativity see Chapter 5 [not currently available in English].

43.   In Beuys's theory of sculpture, *energy* finds its way to *form* via *movement*, and energy transformed into form-seeking movement is the sculptural event. I would add that form-seeking movement is not just "energy," but rather takes hold of it as the fourth (actual) element from the future. I call this the (invisible) child.

44.   These basic demands are not identical with Rudolf Steiner's "law of education," but are interlocked with it in a kind of spiritual logic. In the *Course on Curative Education*, Steiner says that the "I" of the educator works on the soul constitution of the child, the soul configuration of the educator on the child's organism of formative forces, the adult's organism of formative forces on the physical body of the child. And the physical body of the adult, Steiner leaves that open. The conclusion seems close at hand that the physical body of the adult affects the "I" of the child. This is where Steiner's law of education turns itself inside out, and where its challenge lies. What would it mean for the physical body of the adult to affect the "I" of the child? What is the physical body without the body of formative forces? Substance. How can substance "have an effect," or be subject to the effects of the *others'* organisms of formative forces? Steiner has given us a riddle of perhaps unfathomable importance.

45.   J. Beuys/Friedhelm Mennekes, *Beuys on Christ*, Düsseldorf 1989 [not currently available in English].

46.   In Rudolf Steiner's *Collected Essays on History and Cultural History, 1887–1901*, GA 31. The fundamental law of sociology reads as follows:

"In early states of culture, humanity strives for the emergence of social fellowships; the interest of the individual is initially sacrificed in the interest of these fellowships. Further development leads to the liberation of the individual from the interest of these associations and to the free development of the needs and forces of the individual.

"That means that if one does not want to work against the lawful course of the development of culture, society must yield more and more to the conditions of the single person, and thus more and more stress individual freedom over the well-being of the collective. The impregnation of the social organism with the forces of individuality leads to the HUMAN BEING, the social sculpture. The actualization of this principle is today identical with the issue of education and child rearing. It must strive, more consequently than ever, for 'the liberation of the individual from the interests of associations (i.e., society).' Evolution is consummated out of the center of the essence of the child. The directional impulse of juvenile hope is the directional impulse of cultural history. Period. Anything else leads to stagnation."

47.   Cf. on this topic Henning Köhler, *Jugend im Zwiespalt (Youth in Conflict)*, Stuttgart 1994, "The Three Fundamental Expectations of the Childhood Soul" [not currently available in English].

48.   It may put some readers off if I assign the *principle of goodness* to the working world, of all places. But please consider that *active love of one's neighbors*—if one thinks it through clearly— means *working for one another*. Whether goodness can become a sweeping formative force in the social organ-

ism or not depends to a large extend on what will be understood as work in the future. Will it be considered an exertion of force and/or the application of one's abilities for the purpose of earning money, or the exertion of force and/or the application of one's abilities as a gift (!) to one's fellow humans, out of a self-understood responsibility for all people? The increasing social frigidity is not least the result of the unblessed *concept of gainful employment*. This notion foists upon work a central motif and motivation that is entirely foreign to it, and couples it one-sidedly with egotism, which in turn causes it to lose its dignity. The fact that *in truth*—that is, as seen from the primal phenomenon—the working human being follows the principles of *mutual help, sharing, and giving,* and that healthy circumstances can only come about within the working world once he arranges his inherent principles according to *these,* this fact does not live within the general awareness. But that will have to change. Cf. on this topic also Christof Lindenau, *Social Threefolding, the Path to a Learning Society* (*Soziale Dreigliederung, der Weg zu einer lernenden Gesellschaft*), Stuttgart 1983 [not currently available in English].

49.   It was likely not Beuys's intention to underscore *this* particular connection. He looked much more upon the event of death than on birth, conception, and incarnation; upon the cross than on the crib; upon Golgatha more than upon Bethlehem. But on the other hand, I have the impression that he *was* THE CHILD in a tremendous way. Perhaps he was so to such a degree that there was not much for him to say on the subject. At any rate, the idea of childhood is so *graspable* in the expanded concept of art that Beuys would surely not have contradicted the statement that "pedagogy is a central aspect of the social sculpture."

50.   Steiner himself rose to this challenge. His pedagogy is the educational and scientific consequence he drew from *The*

Philosophy of Freedom. Or, vice versa, grasping the occurrence of incarnation in living thinking ("the idea of childhood") is the confirmation of ethical individualism. Precisely speaking, ethical individualism *is* the idea of childhood, that is, its formulation in philosophical terms. Reading the *Philosophy of Freedom* with this in mind as a question yields unfathomable revelations: Steiner is describing the ESSENCE OF CHILDHOOD without naming it as such. He is describing the *individuality.*

51.   Johannes Stüttgen speaks of the "original, concealed point of departure of 'sculpture' (as) development of a higher nature, which aims at society as a *Gesamtkunstwerk*" (in: R. Rappmann, ed. *Denker, Künstler, Revolutionäre* [*Thinkers, Artists, Revolutionaries*]), Wangen 1996 [not currently available in English].

52.   Cf. Chapter 12, "The Child in the Context of the World."

53.   Viktor E. Frankl, quoted after Elisabeth Lukas, *Psychological Care of the Soul*, Freiburg 1996, [not currently available in English].

54.   Help in refusing to adjust as a pedagogical mission? Decidedly! We must encourage children to be disobedient, so that we can receive from them the proper impulses for pedagogical practice and social future. Every educator ought to feel obedient children to be an expression of an educative failure on his part. *The teacher who stands before a well-behaved, diligent class, is committing grave pedagogical errors.* Otherwise, he would not be standing before a well-behaved, diligent class. "Authority" is written on an entirely different sheet of paper. Children dare to creatively oppose an authority whom they love. They grow in creative resistance through him. A "no" becomes a world-important, respectful, tender possibility.

55.   Prior to a session of this kind, the counselor has acquainted herself thoroughly with the domestic circumstances and life history of the child in question, and has also played

for several hours with this child. Even though the minutes of the actusl sessions have been altered, similarities of this fictionalized conversation with talks that have actually taken place are unavoidable.

56. On this topic (creativity, giving, love, and so forth) my book *Eros als Qualität des Verstehens. Über die gemeinsame Quelle von Kreativität und Zärtlichkeit (Eros as a Quality of Understanding. On the Common Origin of Creativity and Tenderness)* was published in 1997 by FIU Publishing Company [not currently available in English].

57. Miriam's parents found out, for example, that it contributed much to peace in the family when certain rituals, such as fairy-tale time, or playing and painting together, were coupled with the discussion of everyday issues. Many a touchy matter was able to be solved peaceably by this means. Furthermore, it proved helpful to avoid the command tone and to present what was to be demanded or prohibited in a narrative or communicating way, calmly, friendly, with body contact whenever possible, hence consciously establishing a situation of closeness. To avoid misunderstandings, it should be pointed out that only segments of conversations have been presented here. Parents naturally also receive other practical recommendations and indications in the course of a counseling process of this kind.

58. Rudolf Steiner, *The Fundamental Spirit and Soul Forces of Art as an Education*, 1922.

59. The etheric proximity and second coming of Christ emphasized repeatedly by Rudolf Steiner are opposed by the constellation of the "force field of cold" described in Chapter 6, and the "cold machine" described in Chapter 13 in such a way that it is chiefly the *children* who become the target. This is no accident. At present, human love is supposed to be destroyed in its core. For this reason, we must take hold of it in its core, as the idea and the ethics of childhood.

60. C.f. Chapter 4.

61.   Two things will need to be brought forward if we want to prevent ever greater catastrophes in the life of the body social: 1) the insight that all political and economic decisions pertaining to the future must have justification based on the ethics of childhood; 2) the formation of appropriate committees to guarantee this. Education will have to keep watch over politics, even though such a notion as yet sounds utterly utopian.

62.   C.f. Chapter 5.

63.   C.f. Chapter 6.

64.   For example, children are brought to us again and again in our educational counseling center who strictly refuse to come into contact with *water* any more than absolutely necessary. I recall a little boy who was always preoccupied with books even though he was unable to read, and was deeply upset if a book sustained any damage. I have met several children who, until they were seven or eight years old, had a completely unexplainable "hysterical" relationship to other people's hair that vacillated between despair and fascination. Others occupied themselves for years chiefly with hedgehogs, or rabbits, or hands, or noses, or trees, or with certain odors. From where do these affinities/antipathies come? The children were certainly not raised to have them.

65.   C.f. note (to the minutes of the conversation about Miriam M.).

66.   This cremark should not be construed to say anything against psychotherapy or curative institutions or homes. The author has himself worked for years in boarding schools for curative education and has for years been active in outpatient support for children with special needs. He owes his fundamental conception of the impulse of curative education to the indications of Hans Müller-Wiedemann.

67.   Groener/Kandler (eds.), *Seven Thousand Oaks, Joseph Beuys*, there: Johannes Stüttgen [not currently available in English].

68.   C.f. Chapter 4.

69.   C.f. Chapter 7.

70.   As an introduction: Toshimitsu Hasumi, *Zen and the Art of Writing Poetry*. Bern/Munich/Vienna: 1986 [not currently available in English].

71.   Pertaining to the cosmic creative aspect of perception: Henning Köhler, *Der Mensch im Spannungsfeld zwischen Selbstgestaltung und Anpassung*, Esslingen 1995 [not currently available in English].

72.   The practical indications given throughout this book are meant as *examples*. Whoever has understood what is at the core of the matter will be able to develop his own exercises.

73.   C.f. Chapter 11.

74.   Rudolf Steiner describes the "configuration of the human members" in his basic anthroposophical writings and many lectures as a fourfold configuration (physical body, ether body, astral body, I) that unfolds out of the triad of thinking, feeling, and willing. In the "higher human being," which everyone carries in himself, the soul faculties and the members are transformed toward the ability to love. WHO does the transforming? THE CHILD! It takes higher attentiveness not to fall into schematics when occupying oneself with this conceptual world of Steiner's; schematics would not suit it at all. One can best protect oneself from such schematics by always developing one's *own* concepts, which have been derived directly from the phenomena, in the sense of the above described creative formation of hypotheses, and not allowing oneself to be intimidated by the unavoidable philistines, who then naturally always ask: where is that written in Steiner's works? Happily, if one has been stimulated by *nature* of Steiner's mind, one can arrive at lots of things that Steiner did not himself *say*. A number of things about the study of the configuration of the human members has been explained in my first two books *The Quiet Yearning to*

Return Home and *Youth in Schism* [not currently available in English]. The "four levels" (existence, convention, transformation, revolt) described in my books, (*The Human Being in the Field of Tension between Self-Realization and Adjustment*, Esslingen 1995; *The Biographical Primal Phenomenon, Mysteries of the Course of the Human Life*, Esslingen 1997 [not currently available in English], *The Human Biography in the Light of the Expanded Concept of Art*, Wangen 1997/98 [not currently available in English]) are *not* identical with the human members; neither are they derived from them. There are correspondences, though.

75.   It occurs already in the alternation between sleeping and waking. But it also occurs in any *creative* process. And in love. Only the CHILD can love and accept love. Only the CHILD is capable of creations of its own. Only the CHILD can ask questions.

76.   C.f. Henning Köhler, *Youth in Schism*, Stuttgart 1994, [not currently available in English].

77.   From the periodical *Wege* (*Paths*), 4/94: "Pedagogical principle: if a person comes to you with a question, do not send him away with an answer, but with ten new questions" (Lena Forsberg). What do we know?

Bibliography

Aigner, C. W. *Das Verneinen der Pendeluhr*, Stuttgart: 1996.

Bärtschi, Christian. Aus einem unveröffendichten Manuskript eines Vortrags vor dem Schweizerischen Heimverband über Pestalozzi, July 1996.

Bettelheim, Bruno. Ein Leben für Kinder, München: 1990.

Beuys, Joseph/Mennekes, Friedhelm. *Beuys on Christ*, Düsseldorf: 1989.

Bohnsack, Fritz/Kranich, Ernst-Michael (Hrsg.). *Erziehungswissenschaft und WaldorfPädagogik*, Weinheim/Basel: 1990.

Buber, Martin. *Ich und Du*, Heidelberg: 1983.

Dobertin, Winfried. *Bildungsnotstand. Warum Eltern, Lehrer und Schuler geflrdert sind*, Frankfurt/Berlin: 1996.

Dürckheim, Karlfried Graf in Franziska Stalman (Hrsg.). *Die Psychologie des 20. Jahrhunderts*, München: 1989.

Fels, Gerhard. *Der verwaltete Schüler*, München: 1994.

Feyerabend, Paul. *Erkenntnis für freie Menschen*, Frankfurt: 1980.

Flitner, Andreas/Scheuerl, H. (Hrsg.). *Einführung in pädagogisches Sehen und Denken*, München: 1984.

Frankl, Viktor E., zitiert nach Elisabeth Lukas. *Psychologische Seelsorge*, Freiburg: 1996.

Freud, Sigmund. *Studienausgabe*, Band 1–10 und Erganzungsband. Hrsg. von Uexkiill und Grubrich-Simitich, Frankfurt am Main: 1989.

Fromm, Erich. *Psychoanalyse und Ethik*, Frankfurt/Berlin / Vienna: 1978.

Grasse/Leber in Bohnsack, Fritz/Kranich, Ernst-Michael (Hrsg.). *Erziehungswissenschaft und WaldorfPädagogik*, Weinheim/Basel: 1990.

Groener, Kandler (Hrsg.). *Siebentausend Eichen. Joseph Beuys*, Koln: 1987.

Gronemeyer, Marianne. *Lernen mit beschränkter Haftung, Über das Scheitern der Schule*, Berlin: 1996.

Hasumi, Toshimitsu. *Zen in der Kunst des Dichtens*, Bern/München/Vienna: 1986.

Havel, Vaclav, zitiert nach Neil Postman. *Keine Gotter mehr. Das Ende der Erziehung*, Berlin: 1995.

Heisterkamp, Jens. *Der biotechnische Mensch*, Frankfurt: 1983.

Hentig, Hartmut von. "Welche Schule brauchen wir?" in *Zeit-Punkte* 2/ 1996.

_____. *Die Schule neu denken*, München/Vienna: 1993.

_____. *Bildung*, München/Vienna: 1996.

Hillmann, James/Ventura, Michael. *Hundert Jahre Psychotherapie, und der Welt geht's immer schlechter*, Solothurn/Dusseldorf: 1993.

Köhler, Henning. *Der Mensch im Spannungsfeld zwischen Selbstgestaltung und Anpassung*, Esslingen: 1995.

_____. *Die stille Sehnsucht nach Heimkehr. Zum menschenkundlichen Verständnis der Pubertätsmagersucht*. Stuttgart: 1995.

_____. *Jugend im Zwiespalt. Eine Psychologie der Pubertät für Eltern und Erzieher*, Stuttgart: 1994.

_____. *Working with Anxious, Nervous, and Depressed Children*, Fair Oaks, CA: AWSNA Publications, 2001.

_____. *Das biographische Urphänomen. Geheimnisse des menschlichen Lebenslaufes*, Esslingen: 1997 (in Vorbereitung).

_____. *Eros als Qualität des Verstehens. Ober den gemeinsamen Ursprung von Kreativitiit und Zärtlichkeit*, Wangen: 1997.

_____. *Der menschliche Lebenslauf im Lichte des erweiterten Kunstbegriffes*, Wangen: 1997/98 (in Vorbereitung).

Korczak, Janusz. *Wie man ein Kind lieben soll*, Gottingen: 1983.

Lindenau, Christof. *Soziale Dreigliederung. Der Weg zu einer lernenden Gesellschaft*, Stuttgart: 1983.

Lukas, Elisabeth. *Psychologische Seelsorge*, Freiburg: 1996.

Meijs, Jeanne. *Problemkindern helfen durch Spielen, Malen und Erzählen. Ein Ratgeber für Eltern und Erzieher*, Stuttgart: 1996.

Montessori, Maria. *Kinder sind anders*, München: 1996.

_____. *Frieden und Erziehung*, Freiburg: 1989.

Müller-Wiedemann, Hans. *Mitte der Kindheit*, Stuttgart: 1989.

Neill, A. S. *Theorie und Praxis der antiautoritären Erziehung*, Reinbek: 1969; zahlreiche weitere Auflagen.

Nuber, Ursula: *Der Mythos vom frühen Trauma. Über Macht und Einfluss der Kindheit*, Frankfurt: 1995.

Postman, Neil. *Keine Gatter mehr. Das Ende der Erziehung*, Berlin: 1995.

Prekop, Jirina / Schweizer, Christel. *Kinder sind Gäste, die nach dem weg fagen*, München: 1990.

_____. *Unruhige Kinder*, München: 1993.

Rappmann, Rainer (Hrsg.). *Denker, Künstler, Revolutionäre*, Wangen: 1996.

_____. *Gespräche über Bäume*, Wangen: 1993. Richter, Horst-Eberhard. *Umgang mit Angst*, Hamburg: 1992. Roth, Heinrich, in Flitner Andreas 1 Scheuerl, H. (Hrsg.). *Einführung in pädagogisches Sehen und Denken*, München: 1984.

Saltzwedel, Johannes. "Erziehung in der Krise," in *Spiegal-Spezial* 9/1995.

Schnibben, Cordt. *Spiegal*-Essay, 18/1996.

Sellin, Birger. *Ich will kein Inmich mehr sein. Botschaften aus einem autistischen Kerker*, Köln: 1993.

Singer, Peter. *Praktische Ethik*, Stuttgart: 1984.

Stalman, Franziska (Hrsg.). *Die Psychologie des 20. Jahrhunderts*, München: 1989.

Steiner, Rudolf. *Die Philosophie der Freiheit. Grundzüge einer modernen weltanschauung - Seelische Beobachtungsresultate nach naturwissenschaftlicher Methode*, 1894. Gesamtausgabe (= GA) 4. Rudolf Steiner Verlag, Dornach/Schweiz: 1995.

_____. Gesammelte Aufsätze zur Kultur- und Zeitgeschichte 1887–1901. GA 31. Dornach: 1989.

_____. *Anthroposophie - Psychosophie - Pneumatosophie*. 1910/1911. GA 115, Dornach: 1980.

"Über das Ereignis des Todes und Tatsachen der nachtodlichen Zeit," in *Die Verbindung zwischen Lebenden und Toten*. 1916. GA 168. Dornach: 1995.

_____. *Allgemeine Menschenkunde als Grundlage der Pädagogik*, 1919. GA 293. Dornach: 1992.

_____. *Erziehungskunst. Seminarbesprechungen und Lehrplanvorträge*. 1919. GA 295. Dornach: 1984.

_____. *Die Erziehungsfrage als soziale Frage. Die spirituellen, kulturgeschichtlichen und sozialen Hintergründe der Waldorfschul-Pädagogik*. 1919. GA 296. Dornach: 1991.

_____. *Die geistig-seelischen Grundkräfte der Erziehungskunst. Spirituelle Werte in Erziehung und sozialem Leben*, 1922. GA 305, Dornach: 1991.

_____. *Die pädagogische Praxis vom Gesichtspunkte geisteswissemchaftlicher Menschenerkenntnis. Die Erziehung des Kindes und jungeren Menschen*, 1923. GA 306. Dornach: 1989.

_____. *Heilpädagogischer Kurs*, 1924. GA 317. Dornach: 1995.

_____. *Zur Sinneslehre*, 8 Vortrage, ausgewahlt und herausgegeben von Christoph Lindenberg. Themen aus dem Gesamtwerk 3, Stuttgart: 1994.

Stüttgen, Johannes. *Zeitstau. Im Kraftfeld des erweiterten Kunstbegriffi von Joseph Beuys*, Stuttgart: 1988.

Vannahme, Fritz J. in *Zeit-Punkte* 2/1996.

Zimmer, Dieter E. *Tiefemchwindel*, Reinbek: 1990.